Dare to Live

Finding Joy at Any Age

D1452851

LORI MANSELL

Photo and cover design: Marilyn Ivette Lopez
Vizual Link LLC (vizuallink@gmail.com)

Printed in the United States of America
Published by Braughler Books LLC., Springboro, Ohio

First printing, 2021

ISBN: 978-1-955791-14-4

Library of Congress Control Number: 2021921834

Ordering information: Special discounts are available on quantity purchases by bookstores, corporations, associations, and others. For details, contact the publisher at:

sales@braughlerbooks.com

or at 937-58-BOOKS

For questions or comments about this book, please write to:

info@braughlerbooks.com

Braughler™
Books
braughlerbooks.com

DEDICATION

To all who have been discouraged, stuck in the past, afraid to try something new, sidelined by health challenges, lonely, isolated, or grief stricken over the loss of a loved one, I dare you to open my book.

Dear Richard,
Dare to live joyfully,
Love, Lori

2021

Contents

Acknowledgements

Now is the time to give thanks to the people who made this project possible; those who were instrumental in making my lifelong dream of writing a book come true.

It all starts with my daughter, Julie Osborne, who gifted me with a ticket to the 2016 Erma Bombeck Writers' Workshop that launched my writing career. After the workshop she empowered me to use a computer and taught me other tools to make writing a book possible — even though I was more comfortable on my old Royal typewriter. Julie was at my side every step of the way, encouraging and comforting me through the new technology jungle and all the lost documents. They're probably still in the Cloud, wherever that is. As my number-one cheerleader, she was always encouraging me to keep going and aiming me toward the goal line. This book would not have happened without her.

Because of Julie I was privileged to have her talented editor, Judy Keene, take me on to edit my work even though I was a novice and her clients are professionals. It was a gift for me but a daunting task for Judy. However, her talent along with ongoing coaching and recognition of my progress, enabled the completion of my book and taught me numerous writing techniques while refining my grammar skills along the way.

Credit is also due to Susan Pohlman, a talented writer, coach, and editor, who helped me set up the framework and chapters for the book and got me started. She continually inspired me to tell my story, believed in me, and always gave me positive feedback. I first met Susan at the Erma Bombeck Writers' Workshop where my writing career began at age 87 after I was crowned "Queen" of the conference. Motivational speakers/authors Kathy Kinney and Cindy Ratzlaff placed a jeweled crown on my head and since then have inspired me with their positivity through their "Queen of Your Own Life" Facebook page and Thursday check-ins. They make me feel like a queen and have introduced me to many fellow queens who are continually rooting me on.

As you may have guessed, I like costumes. On the cover you can see how my talented photographer, Marilyn Ivette Lopez, made me look pretty good in my favorite blue outfit. She was also the creative graphic designer for my book cover, website, and logo that I hope you check out at www.DancingGrammie.com.

Of course I am grateful for my publisher, David Braughler, who made the book that you are holding in your hands possible. He took on a 92-year-old newbie who knew nothing about publishing and was gracious and patient as I learned the process. Stay tuned, David,

I'm already working on the next book!

I am overwhelmed by the love of the many family members and friends who have encouraged me through the years, beginning with my family: husband Ed; children (and spouses) Tom (Deb), Jim (in heaven), Scott (Cindy), Mike (Beth), Diana (Webb), Maria (Wayne), and Julie; grandchildren Meghan, Stephen, Jacqueline, Corey, Hailey, Jessie, Katie, Laura, Tony, Jennifer, Jerrod, Emilie, Will, Ashley, Timothy, Megan, Nate, and Carolyn; great-grandchildren Thomas, Connor, Rowan, and Ford.

Finally, I would not be the writer I am today without the ongoing support and inspiration from the Erma Bombeck community, especially Patricia Wynn Brown who noticed this "Erma Virgin" out of a crowd of 350+ workshop attendees. I arrived as a virgin but left as a queen with a promise to write a book — and here it is.

I have truly been blessed by all of these wonderful people along my journey. No one walks alone, and I certainly have had a village of people to help me, along with God, every single step of the way.

Introduction

My lifelong dream has been to write a book. And as I approached 90, I said to myself, "It's now or never." So here it is, my first book, coming to you at age 92. But does age even matter? You may not think so after reading my book.

As you will discover through the pages that follow, I've had my share of heartaches and struggles, but I've emerged as a grateful, optimistic, and joyous nonagenarian. I get up every morning thanking God for each new and wonderful day, knowing they all aren't going to be gangbusters, but I won't give up or allow negativity to creep in.

My story begins at age 70 with my retirement after a 30-year teaching career. The days that followed didn't turn out as planned and were filled with loss and despair. But a new life slowly emerged as well as an unexpected hobby that would change my future forever.

Life transitions happened, ventures were started, cross-country moves occurred, and new activities filled my days. I dared to take risks, some I regretted but most brought joy and also led me back to life. There were seasons of sadness and fear, but I knew I was never alone and God was with me, opening new doors and providing hope for a brighter future.

Life can be so joyous at any age, and for me God saved the best for last.

I dared to take a chance to live my dream. Now I dare you.

~ *Dancing Grammie*

Chapter 1
Dare to Persevere

There he was, lying in a hospital bed in the center of my living room listening to music, sometimes trying to change channels on the tiny television near him — with fingers that refused to work. It was difficult to see my 42-year-old son bedridden in the prime of his life, but I was so glad to have him with me.

"It's about time you had some clean sheets, Jim. I'm ready if you are." This was the drill whenever his aide failed to show up — often, unfortunately — and it took all the strength he and I could muster to do the job. "Grab the bars, Jim, and pull while I give you a push," I'd say as we started. Spreading out the sheets and tucking them in had to be done quickly, before he'd lose his grip and roll back. We'd joke about how good it felt when the ritual was over. "We did it, Mom," he'd mumble with a smile. There were so few things that Jim could enjoy, and a clean bed was one of them.

Playing *Go Fish* was another. "I think I can beat you today if you want to play now," I'd tease Jim after we had finished the bed-making and I'd pulled out the cards.

"We'll see about that," he'd answer as I sat down and shuffled. That simple game from his childhood was something we could enjoy together to pass the time. Later in the day he'd get a sponge bath, another treat he always appreciated.

Jim had been stricken with multiple sclerosis at age 20, but his doctors hadn't diagnosed it until years later. Symptoms including weak extremities and loss of muscle mass throughout his body left him crippled. Researching a cure then became part of my life. Nothing turned up, but I never stopped trying. My heart ached for him though he didn't complain.

To have known Jim was to have loved him; he was a special young man, always there for me and the family. In fact, he was my sidekick at age 12 when my 1-year-old twins, Diana and Maria, and their sister, Julie, were born a year apart. I still joke that I haven't been the same since, but we made it somehow.

My husband wasn't with us then; we had separated before Julie was born. It was a difficult time, but Jimmy, with his older brother, Tom, helped feed and bathe the babies with me every night. Picture three highchairs lined up in a row in our kitchen, with three little ones laughing and kicking six tiny feet, waiting their turn to eat. It was indeed a sight to see! Afterwards the boys carried their sisters upstairs and put them in the bathtub for bubbles and splash time. A story and bedtime followed. When I finally made it downstairs, I thanked God for surviving another day.

Memories of Jimmy pushing the girls around the block in a big old open buggy are also still vivid in my mind — a tall, lanky preteen with glasses and a big smile on his face. Elderly neighbors who saw Jim coming would walk down from their porches to greet him and his sisters. He'd stop and talk as they oohed and aahed over the girls. Those same neighbors had their grass cut and snow removed by Jim; not for money, just to help. They depended on him, just as I did. I'll never forget the time all three girls had chicken pox, and Jim stayed up all night helping to comfort them. He even slept on the floor in front of their door so I could sleep. It was like having another set of arms when I needed them.

To say times were difficult for us while my seven children were growing up is an understatement, but together we epitomized the meaning of the word perseverance. Married after one year of college, then having babies while doing secretarial work from home and — for a few years — completing my degree in education, was a real challenge. Fortunately, an old scholarship was reinstated, and with Jim's help — in fact, with help from all the children in their own unique ways — I was able to complete my studies, become a teacher and provide a better life for us.

Jim never wavered in his commitment to the family; his after-school job at a nearby pharmacy sometimes provided meals for us. Everyone looked forward to his payday, too; that's when he treated us to "pizza night." I can still see him walking up the kitchen stairs with the pizza and the girls running to greet him.

His sisters still remember how their brother surprised them with their first shiny new bikes — bright blue

Schwinns with twisty handlebars. He had all three of the bicycles spread out in the driveway for assembly while his sisters watched eagerly, and when he finished, the girls took off on them down the street. He also showed up with bamboo poles one day to take them and his youngest brother, Michael, fishing. I imagined what a time he'd have helping all four of them at once, but they were beaming upon return. Michael shadowed Jim whenever he could and learned many skills from him. The two of them together could fix almost anything. Jim had a way with the children; they could sense how much he loved them.

Later, when the twins were in college and awarded teaching internships to Oxford, England, they needed to pay their own airfare. I didn't have the money, but Jim paid for their tickets. "It's no big deal," he said, "I want them to go." I could say much more about Jim's generosity and what he did for me and the family.

Then something happened to him after college, which, by the way, he completed with honors using scholarships, summer internships, and working two jobs. Jim began to have trouble buttoning his shirts and doing minor tasks with his fingers. We thought it wasn't serious until his legs also became weaker and started to give out at times.

Doctors had no answer for the problem. Even though he stumbled more often — by now using a cane — he continued to work at a challenging job at the Chicago Stock Exchange until he fell in the street, hurt himself, and had to resign. Jim personified perseverance, never giving up, until he couldn't physically continue.

After trying various treatments that didn't work, Jim went into seclusion for long periods of time. By then, my other sons had graduated from college and moved away for jobs. The girls were still in school but once they finished, Diana and Maria left too. Only Julie, who lived nearby after college, saw Jim frequently and offered her help. I had remarried and relocated from Indiana with my husband to California while keeping in touch with Jim through Julie. It wasn't the same, but he preferred it that way.

Unfortunately, Jim's mental state began to slowly deteriorate with his body, but his diagnosis was still unknown. It wasn't until his late 30s that he was the subject of a neurological study. As a result of this study, we learned he had an extremely degenerative form of multiple sclerosis that affected his body and his brain, without remission. The news was devastating, but I always had hope and prayed for his healing.

About that time I retired from teaching at a high school in California, where I lived. My husband and I had divorced, and I was alone. When Jim agreed to live with me, I was elated. As I mentioned earlier, the hospital setting in the living room and visiting nursing care worked well for both of us.

As the dreadful disease progressed there was nothing anyone could do for him medically. However, we still managed to share some good times. I was confident that someday a drug would be found that would make Jim well again and, of course, my prayers never ceased.

Jim's brothers and sisters visited occasionally. I'll never forget my daughter bringing her 1-year-old son — my grandson, Nathaniel — for a visit and the great time we had just being together. I recall Jim eating an ice cream cone while my grandson was near him and, when no one was looking, the cone disappeared. Our tiny little rascal had somehow snatched it from his uncle and was licking away! Jim also loved to see my granddaughter, Ashley, a toddler then, living nearby. She giggled and laughed whenever Jim played peek-a-boo or patty cake with her. It was difficult for him to do so, but he made the effort, and we all enjoyed it. Those little ones knew Jim loved them and responded in kind.

Our days went by quietly and peacefully, but it became more and more difficult for Jim to get comfortable without pain. Prayers gave me strength to go on as I witnessed his decline. Near the end, Jim had to be moved to a hospice care facility, and I still remember that day with much sadness. All hope seemed to cease when he left what had been our home together. I knew he had to go. I could no longer handle him physically. His body was rigid and shutting down, and he needed full-time care. Jim lingered two weeks in hospice, spent four days in a coma, and then mercifully passed away.

I had never before lost a child, let alone an extraordinary human being like Jim, and it affected me profoundly.

Although I knew he was in a better place, enjoying his reward, I unceasingly mourned Jim's loss. The children left after the service, and I shut down. There were so many reminders of Jim around me; I wanted to leave. I made an impulsive call to a Realtor friend who listed my house for sale.

All I remember from that time was just existing with no purpose whatsoever. I persevered as well as possible even as an offer to buy the house surfaced immediately, making it time to move.

Julie's long-distance arrangements from Indiana somehow made everything happen as it should. The new owners closed on the house and took possession quickly, while she got help to move me and my belongings to an apartment a few miles away from my home.

A chapter in my life had indeed ended.

My children in 1968.
Back row, from left: Jim, Scott, Mike, Tom.
Front row, from left: Maria, Julie, Diana.

Chapter 2
Dare to Discover a New Life

My life had suddenly changed and not for the better. I was alone, grieving my son's death. The apartment I had moved to seemed empty and lifeless. Hope had vanished with Jim. There was nothing to do except mourn; no reason to get up in the morning. I didn't even unpack, so boxes were my new surroundings. The book Julie sent me about grieving offered no comfort. Sometimes I'd turn on the television from my bed to see or hear someone. Nothing helped.

The kids called, of course, and I pretended to be fine. Why let them worry? "I'm doing OK," I said. But I wasn't OK. I was stuck in sadness, and it wouldn't go away.

This went on for weeks until I finally decided to do something about it. My life had been good raising a family while enjoying my teaching career — both of which gave me plenty of unforgettable moments. But perhaps now was the time for me to follow Jim. I had never experienced that type of deep depression before, and it scared me.

One day I actually stepped into the street as traffic approached. I immediately experienced what could be called an epiphany. God's presence engulfed me as all thoughts of taking my own life suddenly disappeared. Walking back to safety I was certain at that moment that God had come to rescue me.

That same day I sought help from my daughter Diana who lived nearby. She took me to her doctor where I received medication and an appointment to meet with a therapist. Over time, as my depression slowly began to lift and become under control, I began to search for something to fill my days. But what?

Prior to my recent depression, my attitude had always been positive. Now, however, even my age bothered me as I considered potential new ventures. "It isn't as if I'm in my 30s or even middle-aged when a change might be welcomed," I heard myself saying. Discouraged and feeling too old to try anything new, I continued with counseling, focused on staying positive, and grew stronger every day.

Finally venturing out and visiting the local senior center, I began my search for something to keep me busy. "How am I going to fit in here?" I asked myself. The seniors who were painting looked like they were turning out master-pieces — I couldn't draw a straight line! The sewing group appeared to be making blouses — I'd never even attempted a pattern before. Next I found the bridge players. They looked so serious and intense — I'd never survive a match.

Just as I was about to leave, a group of silver-haired women approached me and asked if I could tap dance. I almost laughed in their faces. Not only had I never tapped, I was clumsy and awkward the last time I casually danced at a wedding. (My partner said I just needed practice. I knew he was just being nice.)

"We need tap dancers to fill in for the girls who are retiring," one woman said. "We'll show you the steps and practice with you three times a week." Another woman added, "I didn't have any experience tapping before, but now I'm in the shows. You'll love it, Lori." Eight friendly women were urging me to join them. How could I refuse? Besides, their enthusiasm felt good, so I told them I'd give it a try.

Tapping was very challenging at first. The instructor asked me to get behind one of the dancers and try to copy her steps. "That sounds doable," I reasoned, "but I'll be lucky if I ever master an entire dance." With the frequent practices, I could repeat the steps before forgetting them but really struggled to put the dance together.

In time, the women's encouragement and friendliness improved both my dancing and mental state. "You're doing so much better, Lori," they would say. "Your efforts are paying off." Their kind messages empowered me to keep trying.

Finally, success arrived! My shuffle-ball-changes and time-steps were polished and ready to shine in the shows for The Spotliters, as the group was called. I couldn't believe it at first, and I was excited. But even though I hesitated to perform, focusing on the positive helped me to move on.

My first appearance was tap dancing to a song called "Don't Fence Me In," dressed in a cowboy shirt and hat, which I completed without a "hitch." The number that followed, however, required the use of a cane while tapping, which was more difficult because I had to focus on both my hands and feet. I tried to hide behind a woman in the front row, but that didn't work for long. They soon moved me to the front, and the cane challenge had to be met. It was. I did it. Praise the Lord!

It became very satisfying to know I could learn to dance after 70 — and perhaps also to accomplish anything else I wanted to do. My sadness began to lift. Life and my attitude were better. Having a great hobby with new friends really helped me emotionally, and it was the beginning of a new and happier chapter in my life.

A year or so later I heard about another dance group holding auditions and decided to try out. Yes, me! Can you believe it? I'd come a long way. Knowing very little about The Hot Flashes, as they were called, I did learn that they had more shows, charged a fee to pay a director and choreographer, and were more "professional." You can see how good I felt about myself by then to even have the gumption to try out.

The Hot Flashes differed from my other group in many ways. I learned that quickly at the audition. Members watched everyone trying out and, as I passed them, someone said, "She'll never make it." The words hurt, but they didn't stop me. In fact, hearing them motivated me to try harder — and I actually made the cut! Leaving, someone said, "It's probably because she could fit in the costumes," but that didn't discourage me either. The music, costumes, and challenging routines motivated me to stay.

I enjoyed dancing in two groups and bragged to my children about it. When they learned the name of my new group, they thought I had either picked up a quirky California vibe or was in the early stages of dementia. I let them guess!

My new group had many shows, with music and tapping from Broadway, in San Diego and the surrounding areas. We wore short, skimpy outfits — some with feathered boas — high-heeled tap shoes, blonde wigs, and lots of makeup. I felt like someone I'd never met before, but it was very exciting.

Dancing with The Hot Flashes challenged me to learn more difficult dance steps, while The Spotliters provided lots of fun and friendship. I enjoyed both groups and became a much happier person and better dancer as well.

Incidentally, when joining The Hot Flashes, the director requested my age. She told me that when a dancer turned 80, she was "retired" and could only go to practices. I immediately subtracted 10 years from my age, just to make sure I would be one of the last dancers standing — oops! I mean dancing.

It's funny now to think about some of the strange things that happened to me while I was a "Hot Flash." My wig fell off during one of the shows. I picked it up, put it on my head, and continued dancing. The audience roared. Another time the little panties under my skimpy costume began to slip down while I was on the stage. I managed to pull them up between steps — many noticed and laughed again. The music stopped once while we were performing, and I was one of the few dancers who kept on dancing until the number ended. We got a standing ovation for our efforts. It felt good.

Still another treasured incident occurred when I accidentally kicked my ruby slipper tap shoe into the audience while dancing as Dorothy from *The Wizard of Oz*. Fortunately, no one was hurt, and the show went on.

About that time, I also tried out and got the part of the older dancer in a community theater's production of *A Chorus Line*. The Hot Flashes came to see the show one night, and they all sat in the front row. To say I was nervous would be a gross understatement. They showed up backstage afterwards with compliments. That performance was my claim to fame as a Hot Flash, and I loved it!

You can see that my life had become very full — complete with dancing and camaraderie. Life was good as I packed my bag and rushed off to shows with The Hot Flashes or The Spotliters. Was this really me? Even at this point, I sometimes wondered.

During this new season of life Dan Moseley's words from his book, *Living with Loss*, began to hit home, "Living with loss is a gift that opens up the future in ways that nothing else can." After much sadness and trepidation, learning to tap at 70 (although I told them I was 60), opened up a new door for me.

In many ways, I danced my way back to life.

Me (bottom left) with members of The Spotliters,
my first dance group.

Ready to tap down the yellow brick road as Dorothy
with a few members of The Hot Flashes.

Chapter 3
Dare to Take Risks

My days were full with shows for The Spotliters and The Hot Flashes. I kept busy and was content with my new life in California, also visiting my children and grandchildren all over the country. That made me happy, too. Out of nowhere, came an unexpected surprise; a good one. I met a man named Jack, a former Air Force mechanic and pilot, who spent his days repairing and flying airplanes. We began dating, and it didn't take long for us to realize we wanted to be together. Several months later Jack and I decided to get married.

We enjoyed each other's company and the good life we had in sunny southern California. About two years later we took a trip to Indiana for my daughter Diana's doctorate award ceremony at Indiana University. The Midwest, with its budding spring flowers and greenery, impressed Jack, a native Californian, so much that he began talking about moving there even after we returned home. Both of us had enjoyed being with my family and knew if we lived in Indiana, we'd see them more often. Julie and her children were settled in Carmel, Indiana; Maria with her family lived in Hinsdale, Illinois; and we knew that Diana and her children would join us sometime in the future. The prospect of relocating was on our minds constantly, but it was a big move.

What really sealed the deal was a call Jack received from a businessman he had known years before. His old friend had just purchased a small airport in Westfield, Indiana (20 minutes from Carmel), and he offered Jack a job as a part-time mechanic. We couldn't believe it. Jack accepted immediately. We felt that this wasn't a coincidence. God must have had a hand in it.

We gave ourselves a few days to think about what had just transpired before sharing our news with friends and family. They were so excited. At first, moving to Indiana seemed like it would be challenging, but things began to fall in place. Our house, along with most of our furniture, sold quickly. A search for what would be our new home was completed over a weekend. And my daughter Julie flew out to pack up 20 dish packs of china, along with all the necessities we would need to relocate. She kept us going when the logistics could have been overwhelming. Fortunately, it didn't take long for us to be ready to go.

We made the trip in a rented truck full of belongings, pulling our car behind on a trailer. I recall our good spirits the morning we left, headed for a new life. I joined Willie Nelson singing "On the Road Again" as we hit the highway.

The cross-country trip, however, was not without harrowing moments. Driving on roads under construction with narrow lanes and then having to turn around was scary. I remember getting out of the truck after we had made a wrong turn to guide Jack from running off the road. The construction workers cheered when we finally pulled away. Maneuvering mountain paths and almost running out of gas later certainly got our attention, too. And when I took the wheel to relieve Jack, our stress levels peaked — I'd never driven a huge truck before! Also troubling was when motel clerks warned us about car trailers being unhitched from their vehicles and stolen during the night. I slept lightly with one eye open every time we stopped. Fortunately, a positive attitude had kicked in before we left, and I also said a lot of prayers along the way.

After three days on the road, we made it to our destination — Carmel, Indiana! When we arrived at Julie's house, she and our grandchildren Nathaniel and Carolyn rushed out to greet us with lots of hugs. They were excited and anxious to move Grammie and Grandpa into their Indiana home the next day, although we had no idea what might lie ahead.

My husband and I were very thankful for Julie's help. She was there as we settled into a lovely house near hers, and Nathaniel and Carolyn were the frosting on the cake after some long, hard, house-settling days. The children even gave us their favorite stuffed animals as welcome gifts — a homemade whale and a huge gorilla.

All of my children collectively surprised us with a new living room couch, recliner, and beautiful cherry wall unit. Our dining room table, washer, dryer, and a storm door were additional gifts from Julie. Everything was new and shiny; we felt like honeymooners moving into a little dream house together.

Besides that, we had fantastic neighbors who welcomed us upon arrival. Our home was on a cul-de-sac where most of the residents were good friends, working and partying together. We had potlucks and garage sales often; and I'll always remember one of the men taking our garbage can to the curb, cutting the grass, and running the snowblower on the sidewalk when Jack was unable. "Thank you, God, for these neighbors and all our blessings," was one of our daily prayers.

We had planned to start a volunteer entertainment group in Indiana when we arrived, so we met with the administrator of the local senior center right away. She liked the idea but could offer no help in recruiting people to join.

Soon after that, Jack had a serious accident. He was working in our attic, and as he started to descend, he fell to the concrete garage floor 12 feet below. His pelvis, arm, and leg were broken; he also developed heart problems and went into shock. As a result, Jack had several surgeries and remained inactive for months. Serious health problems plagued him the rest of his life.

Jack was no longer able to accept the job opportunity at the airport, but we had plenty of good reasons to stay in Indiana. We were extremely happy living near my daughter and grandchildren and next to our caring neighbors. Maria, one of my twin girls with four of my grandchildren — Jennifer, Jerrod, Emilie, and Will — was only a two-hour ride to the Chicago suburbs where they lived, and Diana, with her children — Ashley, Timothy, and Megan — would be joining us in Carmel in a few years. Positive attitudes really made a difference for us at that time. "We're going to have a happy life here," we'd often say. And we did.

Sometime later, even though Jack was still unable to help, I managed to gather four people together when the senior center administrator called and asked me to put on a show for an annual event. I immediately accepted, thinking this might be an opportunity to attract more volunteers to join our new group.

We performed a simple program: a few sets of popular songs from the 1950's and my "Boogie Woogie" tap number to honor the veterans who were present. We also told a few jokes seniors could relate to, and that was it. The audience's applause assured us they liked it. However, the best thing happened after the show, when people approached us who wanted to become part of the group. "I only sing in the shower, but this seems like it would be fun" and "No one lets me sing at home" were just two of the reasons newcomers gave for joining. I didn't tell them, but we took anyone who showed up!

Jack still wasn't completely healed. However, I began putting together seasonal shows for the group, which we named "The Prime Life Follies." Our plan was to visit local senior communities weekly to entertain their residents. My husband became the announcer as soon as he was able, and our life in Indiana took on new meaning. We were giving to others and not focusing solely on ourselves and my husband's health problems. There was an opportunity every week to share fun and laughter with our audiences and become friends with them, too.

Learning to tap dance when I was 70 has served me well. I never expected to have my own group continuing into my 90s, but it's still working just fine. It's been 19 years since the Follies started. At one time there were 15 members: singers, dancers, keyboard, guitar, and violin players. We often had two or three shows a week during the holidays and even expanded the number of communities we served. Currently we have seven members: four singers, one dancer (me), a keyboard player, and an announcer. The show still goes on, making lots of people happy — ourselves, included.

Over the years I've thought about how different my life would have been if I hadn't taken these risks. Getting married and moving across the country, along with starting a Follies group, were all new ventures for me. However, they changed my life forever, adding so many blessings. I thank God every day for what he has helped me accomplish.

You too can take a risk and try something new! It doesn't have to be a big move. Just do something you've never done before that could be fun at any age. It's well worth it, you'll see.

The truck that we rented for our cross-country move to
Indiana, with car trailer in tow.

Jack and I felt loved from the moment
we arrived at our new home.

Chapter 4
Dare to Become an Adventurer (or Not!)

The trip from California to Indiana seemed like nothing compared to the adventure now awaiting me in the driveway. I thought it might be a mirage or fantasy; however, after blinking a few times — even pinching myself — it was still there.

A deluxe 45-foot motorhome, with all the bells and whistles — even a slide room to extend the living space — was the new addition to our family. It sat ready to take Jack and I on a cross-country adventure to see the kids and grandkids. After much concern and trepidation, I had let myself be talked into this venture.

How did all this happen, you may wonder? Let's make one thing clear; it wasn't my idea! Jack mentioned wanting to show me an RV one evening at dinner. I knew that, years ago, he had really enjoyed camping and fishing in one of these with his previous wife and their children. But just hearing those two letters, R-V, immediately transported me back to the one and only trip we took after we were first married. "Do you remember our fishing trip in that little RV we rented and what a disaster it was?" I asked him. "We had an army of ants, the toilet didn't work, and the rearview mirror fell off before we reached the highway."

He didn't reply at first, but instead showed me enticing pictures of deluxe models from a magazine saying, "Honey, we can go first class this time with a newer motorhome that has all the bells and whistles." As he attempted to paint a beautiful picture of a fun adventure, all I could visualize were snippets from the first trip. "I can still see the sign in that pitch-black, desolate campground, 'Beware of Bears,' as I walked past it to get to a toilet," I reminded him, pausing his sales pitch.

The conversation continued for days, as Jack seemed to disregard what I said whenever we discussed taking another trip. "If and when we ever travel again, it will be up in the friendly skies to get to our destination, lounging by the pool of a five-star hotel, and driving a luxury car to get around," I told him. But he continued his sweet talk unaffected, showing me more brochures of deluxe motor homes "ON SALE for a limited time only" and assuring me that he'd be satisfied if I would just go with him to look at them.

I weakened, and before you could say "RV" we were entering a showroom with new and shiny motorhomes as big as houses. An enthusiastic salesman met us at the door, eager to show us the "amazing" features of numerous RVs and telling us the special sale TODAY would allow us to put a small down payment on one of them and pay "next to nothing" in monthly payments. His schmoozing went on forever. "It's almost free," were his words as I flashed him a dirty look. Jack was busy climbing into the seat of a big one he liked best, making him look like "King of the Road." He was picturing himself driving down the highway when all I could think of was how much it would cost. A lot, I later learned.

The salesman made another pitch and knew exactly what to say. "I can see your husband really loves that one," the charmer confided, "And you can always buy it today for an incredible deal, have fun with it, and then return it later if you don't want to keep it."

"OK, that sounds doable," I thought. "I'll let Jack get it out of his system with one trip, then we'll take it back." We signed on the dotted line. Smiling ear-to-ear — even whistling — Jack drove the ginormous new member of our family back home. When we turned into our cul-de-sac, neighbors ran out and cheered. Jack thought it was because they liked "Big Fellow" — the name I gave the motorhome — but my thought was that they were happy because it wasn't theirs to care for — and maybe they could just borrow ours once in a while!

Everyone had a tour while Jack pointed out its features. I took that time to call storage yards where we could park our new addition. It was obvious we couldn't leave him on the street. A ticket would just add salt to the wound, especially considering how much money we had already laid out that day. We put Big Fellow at a storage yard later, and I took two Tylenol and went to bed.

As soon as we received the title and registration, Jack was ready to start our first — and what I hoped would be our last — adventure. Checking the insurance papers and filling up the gas tank were next. The insurance part was easy. However, getting gas at a local station caused major anxiety — both the price and the task of positioning the RV close enough to the tanks. Maneuvering Big Fellow was a huge challenge. Just an average-sized area with cars all around required Jack to back up carefully, then quickly twist and turn the steering wheel while moving slowly to the pump. There were some close calls, but the job was finally completed to the tune of $550. Yes, I almost fainted! That wasn't the last of it either, as subsequent gas stops were just as bad. Big Fellow was always thirsty.

After recovering from the shocking gas cost and mapping out our trip, Jack and I hit the road. We stopped and slept at my son and daughter-in-law's house the first night, then continued on our way the next day. I left their comfortable place under protest, not knowing what the future would bring. It wouldn't be like home sweet home, that's for sure. Indeed, it wasn't!

We pulled into a Rest Area and made lunch from the food in our fridge; I made a note for Jack to check the cooling system as it wasn't as cold as the fridge back home. Then later, after it seemed we had been traveling forever, I finally managed to get the King of the Road to pull into an RV park for the night. The plan, at least for me, was to take a shower, make a few sandwiches, turn on the TV, and relax.

What do they say about plans? "The best laid plans of mice and men...." You know the rest. It certainly happened to me. For starters, the shower didn't work.

Jack had spent what seemed like hours trying to connect services. (He was more than a little rusty.) Apparently, the shower problem belonged on my checklist too. After more effort, he did manage to get water to the kitchen sink, and — you guessed it — that's where I bathed!

Sandwiches came next. Jack would have liked a home-cooked dinner. "Next time," I promised. He didn't realize it then, but it wasn't going to happen on this trip. When I finally sat down on the couch to relax and watch TV, I quickly discovered that wasn't going to happen either. The screen had nothing but fuzzy lines, and the sound was just static. Jack thought we might be "out of range," whatever that was. He promised before we left the RV park the next morning, he would have all the "bugs" worked out.

We went to bed after that. There were no complaints about the night's rest we both had; we were so exhausted, we even slept in. That meant that the chores on the list had to wait. Jack wanted to get on the road early, while he was alert. No argument with that. We headed back out after a doughnut and coffee.

But soon after we left the RV park something serious happened: Big Fellow's brakes went out! Luckily Jack was driving slowly down the exit road leading to the highway when it occurred. He managed to pull over to the side and stop, and that's when a truck driver walked over from the park and offered to help. He crawled under the coach with some tools, temporarily fixing the problem, which Jack never could have done on his own. The trucker told us to drive slowly to the next town and find a service station that could replace the brakes. I knew God had sent him and was so very grateful.

The rest of the day was spent in an automotive shop where we waited to get Big Fellow's new brakes. By evening, we were on our way. We learned that the original brakes were somehow out of warranty, so we had to pay up front. Another note for my checklist!

By then a storm was brewing with wind gusts that shook the coach. After many phone calls and hours on the road — along with prayers, of course — we found an RV park for the night and thanked God that we could finally stop safely.

Ignoring the wind, Jack went outside to hook up the water and power. I tried to relax inside, but when he didn't return after what seemed like an hour, I decided to check on him. When I opened the coach's door, it flung open taking me with it and slamming me to the cement slab three feet below.

I remember screaming and feeling dazed and in a lot of pain. Jack came rushing in, picked me up and carried me into the coach. Staying motionless on the couch after taking some pain pills was all I could do. He told me the next morning that I had fallen asleep, and I told him we had to leave. "Turn Big Fellow around and head for home," were my exact words. "This trip almost killed me."

Jack didn't argue, just offered to take me to a doctor. "No doctor here in the middle of nowhere is going to check me over," I insisted. "I'll see one when we get home." Without any more conversation, Jack and Big Fellow put us on the road again — now headed in the opposite direction. Not a word was spoken on our return trip.

Four broken vertebrae were all I got out of our big adventure. The pain and daily use of a heating pad turned into a constant reminder of the disastrous trip. I also learned that my children had made bets when we left on the trip, guessing how many days I would last before we turned around for home. None of them guessed I would last more than a week, and a couple of them bid "after the first night." They had little confidence in their mother becoming an adventurer. They knew me. I had no idea my venture would create so much entertainment!

One of the first things I did when we got home was to call the salesman who sold Big Fellow to us and ask when we could bring him back. "Any time," he answered. However, he also stated — for the first time — that we could only get the price of the coach LESS depreciation. In other words, we lost thousands of dollars just driving it out of the showroom. Surprise! Or should I say shock?

I shouted that he didn't tell us that when we bought the coach, and there was no mention that the brakes were out of warranty either. He acted surprised. Jack had to calm me down as thoughts of running that cheater over with Big Fellow simmered.

Later, when Jack called him, the salesman suggested we try to sell it ourselves. In fact, we had to do that after working the numbers and learning how much we would lose for our first and only "joy ride" if we returned it.

That's when I called my son Michael, a super salesman

who could negotiate with anyone and was very internet savvy. Michael eventually sold it to someone out of state. Don't ask me how he did it, but he closed the deal long distance. We took our last ride with Big Fellow to a family a hundred miles away, who would become his new owners, then returned home on a Greyhound bus — another bad experience I tried to forget.

I only tell you this story so you can avoid a possible disaster like mine. (Of course, a little sympathy for me wouldn't hurt either!) I didn't want to buy that motorhome and should have said, "No." While it's OK to try new adventures, investing in one — especially one that you're against — is another story.

Isn't it funny how you can always look back and say what you should have done? The good part of this story is that it eventually had a happy ending. Both Big Fellow and I survived, and he was probably driving some happy family to places they wanted to see while I healed snug as a bug at home. I learned the hard way that I am NOT an adventurer. And that's OK.

Our first RV trip (and should have been our last).

Chapter 5
Dare to Serve

As I slowly recovered from the RV fiasco, we became more settled into our life in Carmel. Time with the grandchildren and The Follies kept us busy, but an unexpected birthday bus tour opened up more new connections. It all began in Branson, Missouri, at a "rising table."

It was a good-natured trick played on me the first night of our trip with senior members of my daughter Julie's church group. While we dined together, the table crept up slowly as I was trying to eat my food until my chin rested on it. Even though everyone noticed by then and was looking at me and laughing, I still didn't catch on until the waiter appeared with a highchair! Talking so much had distracted me from what was happening. Needless to say, everyone knew me right away.

Over the course of the trip, our fellow travelers became like family. Several days of laughter, while sharing first-rate entertainment and antics on the bus, led to new friendships — and later connected us with places and people to serve.

Our volunteer activities started on Sundays, selling

donuts after church services. We not only got to know more people but became hooked on donuts, too. We also helped at mission fundraising events. Our favorite activity was joining the team that held semi-annual rummage sales.

Every Monday morning we sorted and priced donated items — many of which were unusual and often indescribable. They kept us laughing and wanting more. One time, remnants from a not-so-recent wedding really challenged us. Twelve artificial flower arrangements in massive Styrofoam containers, plastic dinnerware in boxes, tablecloths and napkins — used! And, of course, two wedding dresses with long veils, one of which I had a chance to model at the sale. Sold!

My modeling career did not last long. "Bag Lady" became my new title as the chairman of the women's accessories booth — mostly purses and shoes. (The purses really talked to me, and my collection continues to grow.)

There was also a lot of action at the sporting goods booth. Jack and his new best friend, Paul, kept busy as co-chairmen, and they were notorious for the tricks they played and the way they joked with their customers. They'd line up a row of bicycles for sale and offer free rides to everyone in their area. They also had "bidding wars," as they called them, for "more-than-slightly-used" merchandise.

Once they were given the job of selling a huge calcium-encrusted aquarium no one wanted — even later, when they offered it for free. It was comical to see them corralling customers to bid on it. I did notice that It was gone at the end of the day and heard, but can't be sure, that someone took it off their hands after they paid him a few dollars. Needless to say, no profit was made on that donation.

The Boy Scouts who helped at the sales were also recipients of Jack and Paul's generosity, as the Scouts were able to choose anything from their booth — camping equipment, uniforms, flags, whatever they needed — once the sale ended.

I'll never forget those Monday mornings and the sale weekends. The camaraderie among us was amazing, and it was all for a great cause — to raise money for the church's mission projects. We never knew that volunteering could be so much fun.

Another activity we enjoyed was after-school tutoring. My husband and I, along with others from the church, drove to an old, run-down building in an impoverished area of the city to help children with their homework. One little girl, about 8 years old, casually told us that she had seen a murder one morning while waiting for the bus. It was just another day for her, living in that neighborhood, and it's only one example of how she and the other children with her had to live. "God bless all of them," I prayed.

We were each assigned a child, and a relationship developed that was much closer than that of teacher and student. I had a 9-year-old girl named Harley who proudly announced she was named after a motorcycle. She was a good student and very bright, but I wondered why she worked so fast. One day I learned that when her two older sisters picked her up, they wouldn't walk home with her if she made them wait. They would run on ahead, and she was scared.

My husband tutored a little boy about 7 years old who was polite and excited to learn, even to the point of tackling advanced work. His grandmother stopped to talk every day when she came to walk him home. We could tell she wanted the best for him even though the odds were against the youngster, whose parents we never met.

There were birthday parties, holiday celebrations, and shopping trips downstairs where the children could select gifts for their families that we and others had donated. It was a joy to see their excitement.

Like our sales booth partners, the volunteer tutors bonded and became good friends. It was a sad day when we had to give it up. Jack's mobility became limited after several falls, and I didn't want to leave him alone for the many hours it took to get down to the city and back. Memories of those days will always be special, just like the children we served.

There were many opportunities for serving through the years that not only brought us companionship with other seniors but also provided new hobbies. Hospitals were always looking for volunteers. I took pictures of babies, along with helping their mothers and assisting wherever I could. It was difficult to get a photo of some newborns with their eyes open. They were usually sleeping. (I didn't tell the mothers that their babies were resting now because when they got home, they'd be awake all the time. Take it from one who knows!) My time in the hospital nursery was precious. Holding those little angels even for a short time made my day.

Volunteering in the gift shop was also fun. One night while on duty, the city shut down for a record snowstorm. A call came in for me to lock up and report to the surgical unit. When I arrived, the supervisor asked me to assist in an emergency operation as the weather conditions had made it impossible for nurses to get to the hospital. I didn't have time to think about it and "gowned up" immediately. This was a new experience for me and unlikely to ever happen again. I remember standing near the operating table and retrieving needed items when someone called out for them, and then later helping with clean up. The supervisor thanked me and said I did OK. Despite the excitement of being in surgery, I must admit how much better it felt to be selling flowers and balloons while chatting with customers in the gift shop.

There are many ways to serve others. In fact, it can happen every time we walk out the door. Sharing a newspaper with a neighbor, calling on a friend (or even an acquaintance) who's ailing, or picking up groceries for shut-ins are all ways to serve.

"Do unto others as you would have them do unto you," is an old adage I like to embrace. Making conscious efforts to help those in need is very rewarding. Try it. You'll see!

Sorting and organizing donations at the Second
Presbyterian Church's Annual Summer Sale.

Soon after arriving in Indiana, we launched
The Prime Life Follies volunteer group to bring joy
to local retirement homes. Here I am (center front)
with other members. Jack is in the back right corner.

Chapter 6
Dare to Embrace Reality

Out of nowhere I heard a loud moaning from the garage and rushed out to see what had happened. Jack was lying on the floor, semi-conscious and writhing in pain. I yelled "Help," and my neighbor across the street came running. He called 911 and stayed with us until the ambulance arrived. Immediately, Jack was put on oxygen and rushed to the hospital. I felt numb but pulled myself together enough to drive to the emergency room. It didn't occur to me then that Jack's fall might have caused injuries that would require serious life adjustments or that my role would be shifting from wife into caregiver.

After what seemed like hours, the doctors assured me that Jack was stable. They mentioned concerns about his heart; however, more tests were needed to make a diagnosis. X-rays revealed that his pelvis, left arm and right leg were broken, but they had to wait until the swelling went down to treat them. When Jack finally awoke, he said that his foot had slipped off the ladder from the attic opening 12 feet above. He didn't remember anything after that.

Exploratory surgery was scheduled immediately, but

repairs for Jack's broken bones would be made later. Doctors kept him sedated most of the time to manage his pain, and my days and many nights were spent at the hospital. Exhaustion began to set in, but I didn't realize, then, the toll that it might take.

Surgeries, followed by endless weeks of therapy, dominated our lives in the beginning. Because the accident had also affected Jack's heart, the doctors were concerned that there would be additional problems. We sometimes joked about the fall — we had to — but fear remained ever-present. I remember seeing Jack off to the operating room by saying, "Don't forget your roommate is waiting, Honey," even though I knew he'd be unconscious and struggling for hours when he returned. Often, he didn't even know me.

Multiple operations and then the healing process that followed them kept Jack in bed or in his recliner for weeks. When he was finally able to move around, he used a cane in the house and to get into the garage workshop. Full-time caregiving set in for me: helping Jack with bathing and dressing, supporting him as he tried to move around, and assisting with daily exercises ordered by the therapist. Our days came and went as we gradually adapted to a different life. I found as the days stretched on that caregiving was not for the weak.

There were, however, moments of joy and some breaks in the monotonous schedule. We enjoyed joining my daughter and grandchildren for their activities, volunteering at the church, and getting together with our loving neighbors and friends. Jack even began announcing for The Follies, which became an inspiration for others as our audiences saw how he never gave up. He'd use his cane to go around and greet people, just as we, the performers, did after the shows. He forged on, but eventually a walker became necessary — and then, as he declined, a wheelchair.

My ongoing nursing duties were affecting me although I tried to hide that from others. A friend noticed, however, and insisted I get out of the house. She offered to stay with Jack so I could dance with a group called The Timesteppers. Not only did this new group perform together, but we bonded and supported one another. Having that time to do something I loved while connecting with friends really helped.

Years passed as Jack and I lived out each day one at a time, meeting obstacles and handling them as well as we could. Winter was the most difficult time for us. Jack, a Californian, loved the Indiana snow and wanted to go outside to use his favorite new toy — the snowblower. On good days when he felt stronger, he headed out despite my concerns, and then one icy day he took another fall. That meant another hospitalization followed by treatments. My full-time caregiver role returned, as did feeling exhausted, which became my new normal. When Jack grew stronger again, we established a routine that included The Follies and volunteering one day a week at the church. He was going stir crazy and needed something to do that would be safe. But, unfortunately, Jack suffered another serious accident in the church parking lot, causing complications that put him back in the hospital. Through extensive testing and surgery, the doctors also discovered that he had inoperable cancer that had spread. It was another blow, and I felt exhausted thinking of the long road ahead.

The stress and fatigue of caring for Jack with his new diagnosis hit me hard. I had little energy left for my daily commitments and felt tired and depressed most of the time. One night I noticed swelling in my left leg. Fatigue had been setting in many evenings, and that night was no exception. As usual, I was lying on the couch completely worn out. My leg became so painful that I decided to call the doctor, who told me to get to the hospital immediately.

A record blizzard was blustering outside, but I made it to the emergency room. After a long wait, followed by an MRI, the doctor informed me about a blood clot in my leg that had moved into my lungs and could become fatal. "That can't be true," I said, "I'm never sick." Days later, after treatment, I left the hospital with a warning about my own health issues, which I had never before considered.

Jack's condition worsened quickly. Our days were spent seeking pain-free activities and coping methods that provided more comfort than he had earlier. I had to give up my dance group, and it was a struggle to continue presenting our Follies shows. Jack was in and out of the hospital for various reasons, so being home became a real treat for him. It made it more difficult for me, but I wanted him to be happy and did everything in my power to make that happen. Family, friends, and prayers made it bearable.

Our house had entry stairs and small door openings — not built with handicapped access for a walker and wheelchair. Even taking a shower was a difficult undertaking. Jack didn't want aides helping us, and he refused to discuss hospice. He spent his days talking and visiting with family and friends. He also slept a lot, and I rested then too.

The decision to sell our house and move to a senior living apartment was long overdue but necessary, so Jack could get around easier and also have water therapy, which he loved. I had hurt my back lifting him at home and could receive therapy there too. Sadly, the week after we had moved into our new apartment Jack fell and had to be hospitalized again. Full-time skilled nursing care was necessary after that. He was moved to a facility nearby where he was always glad to see me and his friend Paul who visited daily.

Jack never gave up. In fact, on our final visit he was in the nursing home's therapy room using a machine to work his arms and talking to Paul about a car he wanted to buy. I didn't realize it at the moment but this would be our last time together. He passed away early the next morning. I was in shock.

As I look back now at the years we shared and focus on the good times, I recall the fun we had with his airplane in the early days of our marriage. We participated in air shows dressed in antique costumes to resemble Charles Lindberg and Amelia Earhart. People eagerly took our pictures, while Jack told them stories of his flying days. I also relived the get-togethers with friends and neighbors where Jack was always the life of the party. He was a great Follies announcer, telling jokes between acts and getting even the most serious people to laugh. I could go on and on.

Jack refused to talk about his health problems. Instead he'd get excited about sharing plans for rebuilding airplanes and even race cars, another interest he had. His focus was always on having a better future, not the reality of his decline or approaching death. According to him, everything was going to be fine. But living in denial and refusing help made it more difficult on me. My faith and family support kept me going, and I felt God's presence then and knew the Lord had other plans for Jack.

My role as wife had indeed changed to caregiver during our 15-year marriage, but I don't regret any help or kindness given. It's what God had in mind for me at that time. I'm sure Jack's healthy now and putting on quite a show for everyone in heaven.

Should you find yourself in the role of caregiver someday, my prayer is that you find the strength to accept it and not hesitate to seek help from those around you. I waited too long to acknowledge my own needs and focused only on my husband's until it was almost too late. Share your burden, if and when you have one, with loved ones. Don't try to carry it alone. You'll find their love and support to be just what you need.

Jack and I enjoyed getting dressed up
in vintage costumes for local air shows.

Jack loved dressing up in his tuxedo to emcee
our Follies shows and always entertained
the audience with jokes between sets.

Chapter 7
Dare to Move On

A new chapter of my life had begun. There was no one who needed me anymore, and I didn't have a place to go every day. Jack had passed so there was no rush to be with him at the nursing home. Not only my days, but my life had changed. Follies shows still needed to be created and performed, along with volunteering at the church on Mondays; however, most days and all nights were on my own. A deep sense of loneliness set in. Again, I felt all alone.

Living in a comfortable senior community with amicable neighbors helped. I could knock on someone's door if necessary or greet a resident in the hall once in a while. Morning fitness classes also provided opportunities to be with people, but conversations were limited, and everyone left after they ended. Brief encounters couldn't offset my loneliness. Retreating to my apartment became the new normal.

My husband had spent less than a week in the new apartment, and our home was still up for sale. Moving back, however, didn't seem like a good option. Memories of the daily chores, maintenance for the house and yard, and feelings of isolation in a neighborhood of families remained too fresh in my mind. The decision to stay put seemed like the best option. But how could I make it work — now on my own?

Finding my niche was a priority that didn't come easy or early on. In the beginning, I was grateful for the invitation from my neighbor to have dinner with her and some of her friends, which was my first attempt to socialize. However, despite everyone's efforts to make me feel welcome, it was uncomfortable to enjoy the five-course meal where lively conversation went on for hours. I just wasn't ready for that much socializing. Grabbing a sandwich on the couch after leaving the nursing home every evening had been my daily routine, and it seemed too difficult to change. As I declined additional invitations, they soon became non-existent.

Joining the residents' bridge group was another option I decided to try. My dear friend in the apartment next door once again offered to help. She scheduled "brush up" sessions for me, which really meant going back to my beginner days and starting over. The group turned out to be very competitive, and an opening never turned up. But I did appreciate my neighbor's efforts to get me out of my apartment and connected with the community.

There were times spent with my daughter Julie and her children, a few trips to see other family members, and once in a while, a luncheon or shopping trip, but they were few and far between. My thoughts often drifted back to the past, dwelling on my caregiving days or mistakes and missed opportunities I had made in younger years. I put on a smile as I left my apartment every day, but my heart was aching and loneliness consumed me. It was hopeless, no one could change my new life — take it or leave it. My mind focused on nothing else, and the negative narrative rehearsed in my mind as I headed down this dark path.

Unable to fix it, I finally gave in and allowed my daughter to help. Julie convinced me to meet with a psychologist, as I had done earlier after my son had passed. "It helped then and it could help again, Mom. I'm worried about you," she said. Surprisingly I poured out my heart to the doctor; even spent hours digging into issues that had burdened me for years. Feelings of guilt and shame had paralyzed me my whole life, and it was time to finally get them out. Relief overcame me, and in time the days brightened.

Re-engaging took some time and effort. At first it was difficult to leave the comfort of my couch, but once I started to get together with others, leaving the apartment became more inviting than sitting at home alone. Forcing myself to participate in activities was one of my first steps, and I eventually found myself laughing at times — something I hadn't done for a while.

Certainly there are many of you who have experienced similar grief and loneliness, worn down by caregiving, or even mentally exhausted. Don't wait or refuse needed help, as I did. My resistance to seeking counseling delayed my happiness. Take the first step to do something about it now.

In time you may well find a new and exciting life waiting for you, one that will enrich your days. That happened to me. An unexpected venture began with a Christmas gift from my daughter that changed my future forever. You'll see what that gift was when you turn to the next chapter!

Julie and I on Mother's Day in the lobby of my new retirement community, The Stratford.

Our Follies group after Jack passed away.
The show must go on.

Chapter 8
Dare to Start a New Career

It was a life-changing gift. At the time, I didn't know what a lasting impact it would have — on new friendships, a dream fulfilled, and an unexpected career change at the age of 87. A weekend trip with my daughter Julie to the Erma Bombeck Writers' Workshop in April of 2016 was how it all began.

Julie, a published author, knew that my lifelong dream had been to become a writer, so she bought me a ticket to attend the workshop with her. Erma Bombeck's books had always been a treat to read when I was raising my family. Her humorous accounts of daily life with young children had helped me through some tough times, and my favorite, *If Life Is a Bowl of Cherries, What Am I Doing in the Pits?*, is one I still pull off the shelf today. Attending the workshop allowed me to revisit Erma's stories with working authors.

When we arrived for the conference at the hotel lobby, I immediately noticed the attendees unloading boxes of books and talking to friends about their "new one." I felt somewhat intimidated as we registered, unpacked in our room, and prepared for the evening activities. Julie and I always had fun together, so I decided to just relax and enjoy myself without serious thoughts of a new career, especially at my age.

We headed downstairs for the cocktail hour before going to the ballroom for dinner, and I couldn't help but notice how everyone seemed to know each other. Julie and I were "Erma Virgins" — first timers at the workshop — but as we mingled with other attendees, we very quickly felt at ease. After having a delicious dinner and enjoying a headliner comedian, we retired to our room to plan the weekend's schedule.

The first day took us in different directions. Julie attended workshops for authors needing publishing information, and I selected classes for the novice writer seeking basic skills. My classmates showed much more promise than I did. When we wrote a few lines for the instructor, they immediately volunteered to read their offerings while I tried to hide. The whole morning was a blur of information, but it also brought lots of goodies and handouts for my "Erma" bag. By the afternoon exhaustion was setting in, but the workshops continued. Repeated trips to the snack table kept me going as I attended sessions on "Finding Your Voice," "Humor in Writing," and "Building Your Platform on Social Media." I took lots of notes; however, they didn't sink in at the time. For years, family members had encouraged me to use what I called "The Facebook," but I had never been brave enough to try it. And after the social media session,

I was even more clueless and confused. A nap was in order, as was more chocolate for now and dessert later that night.

On day two I decided to stick close to Julie, and she helped explain and simplify many of the lessons. A familiar overwhelming feeling returned, and I could hardly wait for lunch. We both arrived late to the cafeteria, just in time to hear my name called to go to the podium. Maybe they were acknowledging the oldest attendee at the workshop? What else could it be? Arriving on the stage, Kathy Kinney (aka Mimi from *The Drew Carey Show*) with Cindy Ratzlaff (former marketing executive with Simon & Schuster) placed a rhinestone crown on my head as the MC announced the "Queen" of the workshop. It was me! I looked at Julie in disbelief. Before long people were cheering, bowing, and curtsying. When asked to say a few words to my subjects, I stepped to the microphone to acknowledge this great honor and to encourage the 350+ attendees. Then, promising to return as a published author at the next workshop, I ended with the words, "It's never too late!"

What just happened? Hundreds of people heard me make that commitment. It suddenly dawned on me that my childhood dream could actually be coming true. I wanted to go home and start writing immediately, but before leaving we had an unexpected encounter in the hallway. It was the Bombeck family. What a thrill to top off the weekend! Feeling excited all the way back to Indiana that evening, ideas for my first story started spinning in my head.

I awoke early the next morning to get started, with crown firmly in place on my head, and reached under the bed for my typewriter to begin this new journey. Before the paper was even in the machine, however, my daughter arrived at the apartment and stopped me, "You can't use that typewriter, Mom. Get out the computer I gave you two years ago. You must use that to be a writer."

Needless to say, I was devastated, responding, "It's impossible for me to learn how to use a computer at my age." Julie didn't argue but sat down at the table with me and the computer and turned it on. If I was to become a real writer, there was no turning back.

It's difficult to estimate how long it took, or how many technology crises occurred, before I could produce anything, let alone a story on that computer. My daughter couldn't possibly count the number of desperate phone calls she received when I hit the wrong key or deleted a whole page by mistake. The agony continued. However, the writing did too.

Surprisingly, I eventually finished a story and, with help from an outstanding editor, submitted it for the *Chicken Soup for the Soul: Grandparents* book — and it was accepted! The story, "Me and My Shadow," was an account of teaching one of my granddaughters to dance and how it inspired both of us to continue performing — even until today. Being published with other professional authors was the first step to a dream come true.

You might wonder what happened after that. For starters, I had a book signing. Yes, me! Friends and even people

I hardly knew bought the book that included my story — I actually sold out of my supply! The local newspaper's photographer took my picture, and their reporter wrote an article. It was surreal and actually lots of fun. All the relatives received books for Christmas. I was famous in the family and my retirement community — and, well, I loved it!

Something like this could happen to you. It may not be launching a new career in writing, but it could be a dream from your past or something you have always wanted to try. I met a senior who finally achieved her goal of belly dancing in her 80s. It wasn't pretty; however, it was something she had always dreamed about doing, and I applauded her. Think about it. What is something you've always wished you could do? Who knows what could happen!

Who would have guessed I would become a writer (and a queen) at the age of 87 — and learn how to use a computer!

Being crowned Queen at the 2016
Erma Bombeck Writers' Workshop.

Julie and I were "Erma Virgins" as
first-time attendees of the workshop.

Chapter 9
Dare to Tackle Technology

Royal had been with me since I was a teenager, always dependable and ready to serve. Now she was gone, whisked away without warning or even a "goodbye." How would my writing career begin without her? You see, Royal was my typewriter.

Guess what sat on the table as her replacement? That's right, a computer; one that had laid dormant for years. My daughter Julie gifted me with it when everyone was caught up in the new technology wave, yet I never went near it. But now, if I wanted to become a writer, it was time to make a change — and to tackle this new technology.

I noticed many differences even before tapping a key. With Royal all I had to do to get started was to give her a piece of paper, roll it into place, and type. She didn't ask for anything. This new machine had a blank screen and then words were supposed to appear on it when I started typing on something called a keyboard. It was confusing — no — overwhelming! How could I, a computer virgin at the age of 87, ever understand it, yet alone master it?

Well, I immediately realized that I couldn't do it alone.

Julie came to the rescue as I sat down to begin — and then countless additional times down the road. She watched over my first steps on the new machine, which actually produced a blank page for my story. In order to share my work, she showed me something called Google Docs — whatever that was — and walked through the steps to use it again in the future. Which, of course, I immediately forgot. She also reviewed the keyboard with me, pointing out the "delete" button that would correct mistakes. No more white correction paper or Wite-Out needed; I had an electronic eraser at my fingertips that would become indispensable. Maybe this new computer wouldn't be so bad?

Once I understood the basics — turn it on, open a new document, use the keyboard — it was time to write. The lines of my first story magically appeared on the screen, and I rejoiced. Then later, after what seemed like hours of typing, those same words suddenly disappeared. Nowhere to be seen! An urgent call went out to my daughter who calmed me down and said I had probably hit the "delete" button by mistake. She somehow "restored" the page and the writing continued. When it was time to stop for the day, another call was required to review how to save documents. She explained the "Drop Down" option in something called a "Task Bar" along the top of the computer screen where it said "Save As." Wow! That was a lot to learn in a single day. I was fatigued. And ready to drop down myself — in bed!

What came next? More of the same. I just kept showing

up to my computer every morning, and Julie gave me new tidbits of learning along the way. Remembering the advice of a leader at the Erma Bombeck Writers' Workshop, "Write every day; put something down," that's exactly what I did. The journey continued, along with daily calls to you know who to fix whatever had gone wrong. The computer wasn't my friend yet, but we had to make this relationship work if I was to become a writer. My biggest problem was losing not only pages but finished stories or "documents," as they were called. I sent out an SOS almost daily for the many missing documents — and still have no idea where they ended up. Sometimes Julie could find them; other times they were lost in "cyberspace."

Because Google Docs continued to be a struggle no matter how hard I tried, we decided to try a new approach and headed to the Microsoft store to rent something called "Microsoft Word." It is considered the gold standard of word processing and supposed to be easy to use. It also came with "technical support" when necessary. We left with a rental agreement and a new tool to try. I was so pleased to be able to call someone else and not bother my daughter with every issue.

However, the struggles continued. Calls went out to Microsoft technicians daily, prompting them to log on to my machine to see the problem and solve the immediate crisis. But often, unfortunately, more confusion set in, and I ended up calling my personal support hotline — you know who. After months of difficulties, Julie suggested purchasing an Apple computer like hers, making it easier for her to see the problem and solve my issues. "Your documents will be in the Cloud, and I'll be able to access them." Cloud? Clueless again! Will someone please return Royal?

So off we went to the Apple store to purchase a new computer, naming him "Apple" so he could feel more at home. After all, we were stuck with each other. I still missed Royal of course, but knew I had to forge on — it's not good to live in the past.

There were many things to learn even though the basics remained the same. We gradually became comfortable with one another, and Julie could solve problems easier, which saved a lot of time and frustration. Gradually I began to find my groove, learning about the Cloud and how it was like a huge filing cabinet. My documents were now in this filing cabinet somewhere in the universe — no longer lost in cyberspace. (Still don't know where that is.)

Each day it got a little easier as I found a new routine. In fact, with Julie's help and God's of course — along with an excellent editor — my first story was published in the *Chicken Soup for the Soul: Grandparents* edition, as I mentioned in the last chapter. My dream to become a writer was actually coming true!

Gradually, as I continued to write every day, my computer knowledge also expanded. Email made it possible for me to communicate with friends and family and even see photos of my children, grandchildren, and "greats." Family members had been after me for years to use email, and it was finally happening. Feeling somewhat empowered, I decided to try something even more intimidating: "The Facebook."

As its popularity grew, I felt in the dark when people talked about it. "Social media" was like a foreign language to me, but I knew that The Facebook was a great way to stay connected with friends and loved ones, so why not give it a try? Even though I read a guidebook for seniors, it was still confusing.

That's when an "Apple technician" entered my life to help me — or so I thought. The first time I logged on The Facebook he popped up on the page and offered ongoing services for free. All he needed was my contact information and a check for $250, which would later be refunded after my account had been set up. "It's just a temporary fee," he said. I was delighted! Just think, an Apple technician at my disposal with no cost to me. He was so friendly, even made small talk, asked how I liked my computer, and reassured me that there would be someone at my fingertips 24/7. Then the man who I considered to be a gentleman very politely asked me to write a check and make a copy for him on my printer. I had never heard of that before but, after all, he was an Apple technician and sounded so professional and was eager to walk me through every step.

After I sent a copy of the check, he began asking for more information such as my Social Security number, passwords, etc., and it dawned on me — FINALLY. He was a scammer and I needed to hang up, stop payment on my check at the bank, and alert them of any future activity.

The experience had a happy ending, thank goodness.

My check was cancelled and no other charges appeared. He did have the nerve to call me later, however, and before hanging up, I gave him an earful. It's a fact that scammers take advantage whenever and wherever they can, especially with seniors. My experience taught me a valuable lesson: Don't tell strangers anything no matter how nice they seem, and when they ask for money, hang up.

Despite my bad experience on The Facebook, it has been a great way to stay connected especially during the pandemic. I enjoy reading messages from friends and family and seeing their photos. Making comments under posts is fun too, and I have even learned to write my own. But dangers lurk at every corner. The ads for products that pop up are tempting, but my daughter has told me never to buy them. I'm not even supposed to click on them. Darn it!

Not that I want to brag, but I've come a long way since my separation from Royal five years ago. This future technical wizard is now even "Zooming." Clicking on an email link (I know what a link is too, by the way) brings it up and takes me to a screen that can be viewed by others so we can communicate face-to-face. It's lots of fun. Credit again goes to my daughter for setting it up and solving endless problems with the camera and sound. (I know how to adjust that now also.) It's amazing to be able to meet with friends and fellow writers this way.

Julie and I even do our weekly "Porchcasts" online when we're unable to be together. We broadcast from something called "Be.Live," which was also a new tool that required training. Each week, we ad lib with each other in front of the camera and then premiere the video on The Facebook. Sometimes I'll even add a little tap dancing which viewers love. After all, it isn't often you can see a 92-year-old grandmother tap dancing on a porch! The goal with our Porchcast is to provide "Positivity from the Porch." Of course, I wear my queenly royal robe and crown, and Julie wears her princess attire. (And sometimes I have a sparkly costume underneath.)

However, we have had our share of mishaps during taping. Several times we lost the sound so the broadcast could only be enjoyed by those who read lips. Once my crown slid off, along with my wig while we were live. My attempts to put them quickly back on were the highlight of the show. Another time Julie's dog, Toto, ran off the porch in pursuit of someone across the street. Julie jumped up and ran after him, and I just kept talking. It certainly livened up that Porchcast. You never know what will happen next — we don't either!

No matter how much I master technology, there is always something new to learn. Due to the pandemic, the bi-annual Erma Bombeck Writers' Workshop was held by using something called a Crowdcast. Emcees, presenters and guest entertainers went virtual for participants, and communication with them was ongoing. With simple directions, logging in and even submitting questions and comments was a breeze. On the first night, I was even "beamed in" by the cocktail party hosts and talked to the 650 participants live. Bring 'em on!

You can tell I've come a long way. And if I can master technology, so can you. For someone who's "all thumbs" around anything mechanical, my results have been much better than expected. I'm still a work in progress, of course, but it's getting more familiar all the time.

My life is much fuller now that Apple is a part of it, and I'm connecting and communicating more than ever. As I learned, don't try to tackle technology on your own. There are too many scammers waiting to take advantage of newcomers. Start by working with a friend who's knowledgeable and can walk you through the basic steps of learning how to use the computer — and take your time. Patience is the most important thing to learn because it will be tried every time you log on. I've always been in a hurry and have often sent stories to my editor before they were ready — and lost many others. Who knows how much time and money was wasted by not slowing down and taking on tasks one at a time. You don't have to learn the hard way like I did.

There's something else I found very helpful. Maybe you will too. I always keep a tin of candy with Hershey's snack bars and baby Butterfingers under my desk for technical emergencies. I learned quickly that it needed to be filled every morning before starting to write. Chocolate makes everything better and helps with writer's block too!

Somehow I've lived to share my technology adventures and haven't given up yet. You shouldn't either. Remember to learn one thing at a time — and practice, practice, practice before moving on. You'll be Zooming before you know it. And who knows, technology may bring you other bonuses. That happened to me as you'll see in the next chapter.

Until then, let's become friends on The Facebook! (@DancinGrammie)

Sitting at the computer to work on my first story (once I figured out how to turn it on!)

Chapter 10
Dare to Commit (Again)

If you had asked me how I was doing after Jack's death, I would have answered "OK." Therapy and medication helped my depression, and I was back to normal — whatever that was. I decided to remain in the same senior residence, which had fitness classes every morning, fun activities and dinner socials with fellow residents. Writing kept me busy, too, as well as Follies' shows and practices twice a week.

However, something was missing; I noticed it more in the evenings. Sitting alone in my apartment after being surrounded by a husband and family all my life left me feeling desperately lonely and longing for companionship. Where could I find that? I wondered. And, at my age, should I even try?

With a gender ratio of 40 to 1 in my residence, it was slim pickings for any single woman looking for a male companion. In fact, if a new man appeared on the scene, he was quickly pursued by a multitude of women. Available men in my building were at a premium. It seemed as if they either had spouses or other friends of the same gender for socializing. The single ones ate dinner together every evening, lingering over conversation for hours and seemed content to retreat to their apartments alone. Many single women did the same and appeared to be happy. It worked for them but not for me. I longed to be with someone; to share my life again.

So, despite my initial observations, I decided to investigate the possibilities in my residence further. As I scanned the dining room in search of prospects, my eyes took in many sights. None of them were good. In the corner was a very obese man in the process of eating what looked like a seven-course dinner. The gentleman seated next to him was bearded and boisterous, both of which were turnoffs. Standing by the bar with no one but his drink, a handsome man immediately got my attention until he ordered another one for an attractive woman who showed up a few minutes later. At a table nearby the likely most eligible bachelor already was surrounded by his usual harem of women. Whenever our paths crossed he was very attentive — even flirtatious — but I knew better. He loved us all. Last but not least was a well-mannered gentleman, someone who piqued my interest. That is, until I noticed his full-time aide appearing with him. It was difficult to see how the three of us could date.

There was one exception to this scenario, however, and I'm excited to mention it. My talented editor, also a resident, had a "premium" suitor pursuing her soon after he moved in. (He wasn't like anyone I described in the dining room.) An extremely busy lady, she wasn't even looking for a man, but they fell in love and were married a year later. They proved that it was possible to find love at this stage of life.

But there was no one for me. As my loneliness grew, I discussed it with my daughters. They wanted the best for me, and their suggestions were interesting. Julie thought my evenings could be spent with my friends who stayed after dinner to talk. "Try to get more involved, Mom, even though you don't like to linger," she said. "At least you won't be alone. You have so many friends there." I responded, "I do, Julie, but it's just not for me. I'd like to go out."

That's when my other daughters, Maria and Diana, suggested using online dating. "What's that?" I asked. "It's Match.com, Mom, where you meet someone online who could be a companion," Maria said. "You like to dance and go out in the evening. You could do that."

"I know about Match and it's not that simple," I answered. "What about the men who take advantage of older women like me? I've heard some frightening stories about them." My daughters assured me that they would check out everyone before we ever met. "We'll see," I said as we ended the conversation, and that was it for a while.

I put the idea on the back burner and went about my business. But Maria and Diana forged on. They continued to suggest Match.com, and I finally gave in and said I'd try it. They set up what was called a "profile," but I didn't know how to use it. The whole process seemed overwhelming, so I gave up before even starting. The girls didn't, however, and they called later to see what was happening. "Nothing," I told them. "There aren't any men still vertical out there who would be looking for an old woman like me. They want the young ones." When Diana and Maria learned I had not logged on, Julie was reluctantly called into action. "I really don't think this is a good idea. I'm not a fan of Match.com, but I don't want you flying solo," she said. "There are too many dangerous people out there."

Shockingly, there was already someone pursuing me by the first time I logged in. He had similar interests: dancing, theater, and the Indianapolis Colts. He also had been an educator like me. Ed, my "match," had tried to contact me after he saw my profile, but I had not yet responded. After the initial connection by email, we talked on the phone for two weeks to get acquainted before meeting in a public place for lunch.

Even though we were both shy and nervous, we spent over two hours together, talking about ourselves and our families. He had six children and taught computer science before retiring. I had seven and had been a math teacher. We never ran out of things to say. My first Match.com date was a success!

Ed called later, and we made another date — this time for dinner. He picked me up in the lobby of my apartment building, bringing flowers and photo albums of his children that we perused together after dinner. Our conversations flowed until closing time when we were asked to leave the restaurant. We obviously had a good time together.

Phone calls, lunches and dinners, casual dates for a walk and ice cream, Colts games at Lucas Oil Stadium, and dancing on Friday and Sunday nights kept us very busy. We both had so much to say and do together, even watching old movies or the History Channel at my apartment. I was not writing as much or getting near enough sleep. But who cared? I was happy.

We were comfortable with each other; it seemed as if we had been friends for years. Sometimes we'd laugh at how we felt like teenagers again. Within six months, Ed surprised me at a Sunday night dance during intermission. In the middle of the dance floor, he got down on one knee, pulled out a ring, and asked me to marry him. People around us cheered.

The proposal was not a complete surprise — he had been telling me he loved me for a while — but it initiated some serious conversations about a future together. We both felt more time and counseling from our priest was needed to make sure this was the right decision for us. We wanted our marriage to be a blessing and realized it was statistically proven to be more difficult for newlywed seniors to live together — too set in their ways was the reason given. Counseling sessions began, and a tentative date for our wedding was set for the next year.

Ed and I both knew the location for our future home was a factor. I continued to rent my apartment, and he owned a house in another senior community. Our homes were 20 miles apart so choosing a place between our locations seemed reasonable. Luckily, we found a new home in a senior community that met our current needs and would accommodate us in the future if we needed extra medical attention. It was located in a convenient area near shopping and anything we would need, so we put our names on a list to purchase a house that would be completed the next year.

A simple church wedding for family and friends had to be planned. My daughter Diana took over the reception planning, and we booked a honeymoon cruise. Our wedding and first trip together were very meaningful. We felt like a couple of kids in love and anxious to spend the rest of our lives together. Who would have guessed that we would find such happiness by way of the computer!

(By the way, I actually wrote our story called "Mom on Match," and it appears in the *Chicken Soup for the Soul: Age Is Just a Number* edition.)

Ed and I helping carry the flag at a home Colts game.

A toast to our new life together on our wedding day.

Chapter 11
Dare to Honeymoon (at 88!)

There we were at the railing of a beautiful ship, with soft lights all around us and an orchestra playing "Moonlight Bay" as we sailed out of the Vancouver harbor bound for Alaska. It was straight out of a scene from a romantic movie. Our honeymoon cruise was just beginning, and we could hardly wait to set sail. Not only were we starting our first cruise together, we were also beginning a new life with each other.

A special stateroom with a balcony and beautiful bouquet of flowers awaited us. Even though my husband Ed had a serious heart condition, he didn't care and swept me up and carried me over the threshold. I felt like a blushing bride. Age didn't matter. Someone on the deck asked if we were newlyweds. I guess it showed, and that made us smile even more.

Later in the cabin together, unpacking our clothes seemed a bit awkward at first. Sharing spaces and deciding whose stuff was going where took a little getting used to — we'd never done this together before, so we took our time, alternating between smooching on the balcony and putting things away. I felt like a bride as I soaked in the ambience of the cabin while the scent of the lovely flowers filled the air. This was all so new and pleasant. "Thank you, God," was all I could say.

Dressing for dinner was fun too. My best dresses were hanging up to choose from, and I let Ed make the choice. "That's what I would have picked," I said to him after he made his selection. "It's my favorite," he replied. We knew pictures would be taken in the evenings, so this would be our routine every night. I didn't care, dressing up had been a favorite of mine since childhood. Ed went along with it — he had no choice.

We ate buffet dinners instead of opting for formal dining so we would have more time for the first-class entertainment scheduled every night. We never missed a show. In fact, one evening we were chosen as one of four couples to play *The Newlywed Game*! After we were picked, I said to Ed, "I'm nervous and don't know what to do," as we headed up to a gigantic stage to compete with three other couples who had been married 25, 40, and 60 years.

"We were married a few days ago," I told the huge audience as I began to relax. The other couples also shared their weddings from the past and then the men were escorted off stage. The host asked the ladies some questions about their husbands: "What's his most annoying habit?" "What car does he resemble when he gets out of the shower?" "What's he got that's large and also what is 'itty bitty'?" and lastly, "Where did you ever make love together outside?"

I gave complimentary answers, such as "Ed doesn't have any annoying habits," "He's a Rolls Royce," "He has a large heart and an 'itty bitty' temper." The last question about where we made love outside really shocked me. Of course, the host was no help at all as he repeatedly suggested places I'd never even think of, let alone go for an intimate encounter. I finally replied, "In the parking lot behind Steak & Shake." The audience screamed. We did kiss a lot there after a hot fudge sundae once, but everyone thought it was something else and went wild.

When the men returned, none of them got more than one of their wives' questions right. Ed was "spot on" about the parking lot behind Steak & Shake and even embellished it a bit. Everyone roared again.

It was then time for the ladies to leave the stage so the husbands could answer questions about their wives. When we returned, I was the first one to answer. "When and where was your first date and tell us something about it?" the host asked. I easily recalled our meeting for lunch at McAlister's Deli on a certain day and talking for over two hours until the staff started coming by to look at us. Ed had the same response.

"Where did your husband propose to you?" was next, and my answer, like his, was "In the middle of the ballroom at a Sunday dance we attended." Another easy one for us.

The one question that shocked me and brought the audience to their feet cheering was, "Tell us your wife's bra size." This one Ed decided to respond with action instead of words, cupped his hands and holding them out in front of him. Again, the audience roared!

Of course, I didn't get that one right, but we won anyway and became famous on the ship — or should I say *in*famous! Everywhere we went people smiled and joked with us, and it was lots of fun. The prize wasn't bad either. We got a basketful of champagne, perfume, and jewelry from the boutique. What a night to remember!

After the shows ended, each night we would head to the lounge where our favorite band was playing dance music we liked, and we never missed a beat — literally. In fact, we won another bottle of champagne one night at another fun contest. We each had to remember when we had had our first dance together and what song was playing. Both of us answered the question correctly and then danced to the same tune for the audience. Being honeymooners was bringing us good fortune and notoriety — and we enjoyed it.

Neither of us were drinkers. Ed's medicine wouldn't allow it, and one drink would put me under the table — or on it! But we enjoyed our time in the lounge every night and met many friendly people from around the world.

Returning to the cabin was always pleasant. Our steward turned down the bed and laid out mints on the pillows every night. He also made animals out of towels and displayed them in the room. We had no complaints about the service. Remember the old cliché "We slept like babies," then apply it to us; we always awoke rested and ready to enjoy another day together.

Breakfast buffet was our daily starter, with the choice of so much good food we had to ration ourselves later. We enjoyed sitting in the buffet dining area and seeing glaciers as we sailed by. It was sunny and welcoming, even in late August. "Come sit with us, newlyweds," was the usual greeting as we got acquainted with fellow passengers and enjoyed the camaraderie there. It was a wonderful way to start another day of our new life together.

A stop at the fitness room for a little exercise came next, and preparations for excursions we had selected earlier followed. That took up part of each day. We always had an afternoon nap and time in the pool, too. Ed was a good swimmer and did laps. I couldn't swim, but I jumped around and enjoyed myself. I couldn't float either; didn't relax, just tightened up and sank to the bottom. Thankfully I always came up!

A land trip followed the cruise where we visited Alaskan towns and villages. The accommodations were rustic but, to be honest, I missed the grandeur of the ship. My words when we had to disembark were "I'm leaving under protest," and it was true. During our time on land, we learned a lot about Alaska's frontier and history before boarding our flight home from Fairbanks. We took so many memories with us from our honeymoon. It couldn't have been better.

If you want to have some fun, relax and get spoiled, you might consider a cruise too. We would recommend cruising to anyone who likes good food and entertainment, service in a luxurious cabin, tours to historical places, and a chance to meet nice people from all over the world. We plan to book again. Who knows, we may see you at *The Newlywed Game*.

Who would have guessed that we would win
***The Newlywed Game* on our honeymoon cruise!**

Chapter 12
Dare to Merge

Still glowing from the wedding and honeymoon cruise that had just ended, I opened the door to our new home only to be greeted by some unfamiliar sights. A potbelly stove welcomed me in the front hall, sitting beneath antique pictures of relatives I didn't recognize and surrounded by little statues sprinkled around the floor. I must be seeing things! I wasn't. Ed was excited and asked how I liked some of his most cherished possessions. It was at that moment that the honeymoon ended. Reality set in. I wanted to say something but bit my tongue and gave him a hug.

We knew our stuff had to be merged, and the challenge would be daunting. His former home had been full of things he liked; so was mine. We both were "savers." (Please note I did not say "hoarders," as some might assume from my story!) As a result, the task of finding places for everything Ed and I had collected throughout our lifetimes was going to be monumental.

I also couldn't help noticing that he had been unwrapping his collection of rocks from all over the world and putting them on the kitchen counter nearby. I had hoped he would have put his tools away in the garage cabinet instead of looking at his rocks. But they were very important to him just as my china was to me. Certainly, it will get unwrapped soon, I told myself. Again, I didn't say anything.

We had left the movers a diagram so they put the furniture in the right places. We were using mine, which my children had gifted me years earlier. Ed offered his children any pieces they wanted, then donated the rest. I was glad to see his orange couch and one of his two faded mauve chairs were no longer in the house — that made me happy, but not for long. "The twins," as I called these chairs, were supposed to go to a new home with his daughter, who lives in Colorado and was driving them back with her after the wedding. (I learned later only one fit in her little hatchback.)

They had been together in Ed's living room and now one would have to sit in our bedroom until his daughter made another trip to get it. (That's another story I won't get into now.) The twins looked and acted like the antiques they were: faded and sunken; hard to get into and very hard to get out of. They weren't called "sunken" for nothing — wedding gifts from Ed's first marriage 60 years ago, they had to go.

Then I noticed that Ed had also unwrapped two 10-foot stuffed swordfish that had hung on his former home's living room wall. They were *not* going to hang on ours; fortunately he agreed. We carried them to his office to be hung later, and anyone who wanted to see them could just look to the left as they entered the house. A large shelving unit was in the office too, which could hold Ed's rocks. We were just getting started.

Next, boxes and boxes of china — Ed's and mine — waited to be unwrapped and put in the cabinet. Before the wedding they had been stored in the guest bathroom's bathtub for safe-keeping, and I could hardly wait to see them again. Ed didn't think all the pieces would fit in my large china buffet; I assured him they would, even though I knew from the get-go that there wasn't enough room for everything. So my secret plan was put into play next, in order to keep my dishes out of storage. After all, I needed to see my china just as Ed wanted to look at his fish and rocks.

While Ed unwrapped the dishes and set them on the table. I put some in the cabinet, then snuck off to the linen closet with the rest. The really big pieces went into the closet and he never noticed what was going on. He was tinkering with his cell phone while he worked; maybe that helped. A large soup tureen was the last item I had to hide. Ed didn't remember that I had gifted him with it before we were married so he would have to handle it during our move. I knew it would return to me after the wedding, which it did. Once it was on the floor of the closet, the china challenge was over. We took a long coffee break after that.

Clothing storage was the next problem we had to solve. Even though I had a very large walk-in closet and Ed claimed two double-tiered ones for himself, our clothes wouldn't fit. Another thing we had in common was that we both couldn't part with our garments. After all, they might come back in style and we wanted to be ready!

I shouted "Hooray!" under my breath as I found the solution. Remembering a stack of empty plastic bins waiting in the garage; we immediately commandeered them for our surplus clothes. What was so great about them was they were shallow enough to fit under the beds. We used more bins for miscellaneous odds and ends, "keepers," I called them. Some even held 70-year albums we both wanted to save. They fit nicely under skirted couches and chairs. Of course, we both hung favorite pictures on the walls later, but our biggest challenge still was ahead of us.

The kitchen involved unpacking and choosing dishes, silverware, pots and pans, and accessories. We compromised on our selections, set aside all the extras for donations, and proceeded to set up the cabinets and drawers for use. A large pantry came in handy too, but of course Ed's rocks had to be moved from there first. (Did you forget about them? I couldn't!)

We never really worked in the garage. It held lots of "extras," most of which would go out to our storage unit. Christmas decorations — lots of them — Ed's extra tools and fishing gear, old luggage, and bins full of artificial flowers for possible Follies shows were definitely headed there, for starters. That would happen another day.

We were fortunate to have the cable company's technician stop by to set up our service while we were merging, so I knew the first night in our new home was going to be a good one. We could watch an old movie or the History Channel, and Ed would bring me my ice cream as he always did. There were some small tasks to accomplish, but basically, we were all set.

As you can see, we planned to enjoy our home, keep what we liked around us and not worry about it meeting *Better Homes & Gardens* standards.

If you ever merge with someone, think of how we did it and then do what's best for you. It's not exactly "rocket science," so just relax and have fun with it. A happy home is everyone's goal. It's not the stuff you fill it with; it's the people inside who count.

**Ed's prized fish are the first thing you see
when you enter our home.**

Chapter 13
Dare to Celebrate a Milestone

As the party wound down, family members gathered while we watched a video of our earlier days together. Children and grandchildren from Florida, Illinois, South Carolina, New Jersey, Massachusetts, Indiana, and even Italy were all seated, and I could feel the love. Baby pictures of my four sons and three daughters graced the television screen, along with snapshots of their school days, graduations, and wedding photos. More pictures of my eighteen grandchildren and four great-grandchildren were also shown, and we oohed and aahed together. It was a very special closure to what had been an unexpected but memorable celebration of my 90th birthday.

It had all begun on Friday when my children arrived to surprise me with a three-day birthday celebration. My son Michael with his wife Beth and granddaughter Jessie were the first to show up when they walked in at one of my Follies shows — I almost fainted, but of course the show had to go on after a pause for some hugs. The audience noticed and loved it. I had told my family many times, "I don't want a birthday celebration this year even though it's a big one. I'm not anxious to let everyone know my age. You know I've been taking 10 years off for a while, and I like it that way."

As my children began to appear, it became obvious that a party had been in the works for months before the big day — my request had clearly been ignored as family kept popping up. Granddaughter Carolyn walked down the stairs when we arrived at my daughter Julie's house. Later twin daughters Diana and Maria, with Maria's husband Wayne and their son Will, showed up. During dinner, my son Tom and his wife Debbie, along with their daughter Meghan and my great-grandson Thomas, walked in the front door. Last to appear that evening was my grandson Nate who flew back from Boston after having been home for Thanksgiving just a few days earlier. My son Scott, who lived in Italy, surprised me the next day. When I looked around the room, I was so happy that my children ignored my request for no party. Being together was a feeling I'll never forget.

Little did I know that there were many activities planned for the weekend ahead, beginning with a family fashion show. After dinner, we moved to the living room for our first series of birthday gifts, beginning with a large, brightly colored bag packed with seven presents. As I unwrapped the first item, Julie explained that it was time to pick out a birthday dress (or dresses) — and family members jumped in on the action. Maria held up the first one accurately dubbed "Classic." Debbie paraded around the next very sparkly, sequined frock I called

"Street Walker." Julie was relentless with a hard sell of "Royal Red." Will modeled "Ruffles" while Nate proudly displayed "Rosé All Day." Jessie's acting abilities came in handy as she dramatically showed off a dress called "Sleeves." The competition was fierce.

And the final dress … (drumroll please). My husband snatched it out of the bag and declared it THE DRESS the moment it was unveiled — "Simple Elegance" was its name. He picked the winner — in dresses and, if I may say so, in women. I would be donned in "Simple Elegance" for my birthday the next day, but I still had no idea that I would be wearing it for a surprise party.

The festivities continued the following day with a family brunch. As we moved to the living room to open more gifts, including a royal robe and golden birthday crown, I knew something was up. Tables appeared all of a sudden when Julie made the announcement that we would be having a party. A few minutes later the front door opened and friends flooded in. The visits continued all afternoon, and tears filled my eyes as new and old acquaintances appeared with hugs. There were three birthday cakes, a table of food, and lots of presents. (I even blew out 90 candles in one minute, before the tablecloth could catch on fire!)

The party continued throughout the afternoon and evening with another family dinner and a heartwarming slideshow created by my talented and loving granddaughter Jessie. And the night ended, of course, with dancing! Oldest son Tom did a few wild numbers with me, much as he had done at former weddings. We rocked to "YMCA" and some other fast numbers as he shouted, "You've still got it, Mama!"

As you know, I hadn't looked forward to becoming a nonagenarian, but after the party, it didn't seem so bad. And I soon discovered that there were incredible perks to being 90.

For instance, there's no worry about getting old in the future. I'm already there. Turning 90 and still being alive is a fete in itself, as is avoiding heart problems, multiple sclerosis, diabetes, and other life-threatening diseases. People also tell me, "You look great for your age." Attending fitness classes every day and staying mobile helps a lot. One of my instructors challenges us with full-body movements to the beat of rap music. I stay in the back row, and let it go! Later a nap is required to recover. Getting enough sleep and eating well are also important for my overall health. And, by the way, my mind is still working, although using the "senior moment" excuse once in a while keeps things fun.

My kids haven't taken my car keys yet. Hair and nail appointments (thankfully more often than to doctors), errands, visits to friends, and shopping keep me on the go and feeling independent. However, they are doing something I've noticed over the years with the elderly; they take my arm when we're walking together. I don't mind; actually get a kick out of it. They almost lift me into the car, find me the best seat in restaurants and theaters, and remind the grandchildren to "help" me. "With what?" I wonder, but it's OK to humor them.

There are many reasons to make me smile these days besides memories of my awesome party. I can spend my time doing what I like to do, not what I have to do. Putting together shows for my volunteer entertainment group that I started 19 years ago can be rewarding. Four singers — who also do comedy — myself (the tap dancer), a keyboard player, and our announcer perform seasonal shows every week for residents of senior homes. We get to know our audiences and laugh right along with them. Learning to tap at age 70 has served me well as the group's only dancer. I should mention that I'm known as "Dancing Grammie" to my family, and they don't have to beg me to don a sparkly costume with a feathered boa to dance for them. Dancing Grammie is ready any time.

Writing stories and books like this one also keep me busy every day. As you might recall, my daughter Julie took me to a writers' conference in 2016, where shockingly I was crowned "Queen" and promised to return as an author. It lit the spark for a childhood dream to come true. It's very fulfilling to sit at the computer every day and write tales that others might enjoy. And my days are topped off by watching old reruns of *Mash* and eating ice cream. Calories don't count after 90!

A lot of good things are happening to me as a nonagenarian, but even more are coming. Keep your eyes open for another book I'm going to publish before I'm 100. I've got a lot more living to do. Remember it's never too late for you either.

Celebrating my big 90th birthday with beloved family
members. And, yes, I blew out all 90 candles!

Despite the hard sell by granddaughter Jessie,
"Sleeves" did not make the final dress cut,
but the fashion show was a lot of fun.

Chapter 14
Dare to Purge Past Mistakes

My weekend birthday party brought great joy and positive thoughts about starting a new decade with many more good days ahead. But it also left me thinking about an issue that needed to be addressed. Now seemed like the perfect time to finally forgive myself for mistakes I had made and the feelings of unworthiness that had burdened me for years. No one knew about them; but underneath my outward appearance of peace and joy, there was a sense of guilt and failure that surfaced frequently without warning — by way of nightmares. Now was the time to remove them from my life, forever. It was now or never.

As I reflected back on my childhood to see when my negative feelings might have started, I realized that they had begun very early in life. My parents, both in their 50s, adopted me during the Depression, and as I grew up I sensed that my presence was a difficult adjustment for them after being childless during their first 25 years of marriage. As they aged, I always worried about them.

We lived on the outskirts of a small town where my two dolls, Big Baby and Patsy Ann, were my only playmates since no other children lived nearby. My days were spent pretending with many ideas up my sleeves, or so my parents said. I recall feeling sad and lonely, hiding beneath the dining room table "mothering my dolls" under the draping lace tablecloth. There were also "hollyhock weddings" with flowers from the yard becoming colorful bridesmaids for ceremonies held on the front porch stairs. I was always the bride.

When I started school, the nuns labeled me a "crybaby" as I couldn't hold in my feelings of compassion for those hurting around me. My classmates picked up on that too. Constantly seeking approval and validation, I became an overachiever who needed ongoing compliments and acceptance, always striving to be someone who was smart and polite and as good as everyone else. As an adoptee, I never felt wanted or worthy as my biological parents had given me up. Then problems with my adoptive parents, who were older and had health issues, surfaced during my late teens. My choices were not the same as theirs, especially when it came to my future husband, but I desperately wanted to please them.

As time passed, I increasingly thought about leaving home, and I realized the only way out without hurting my parents was to get married. (People married right out of high school in those days.) They had someone in mind for me whom they liked and who pursued me constantly, and they encouraged our dating and future marriage. They liked his family too which was important, especially for my mother who frequently quilted and embroidered with his grandmother. He was not my choice and had problems of his own, but I married him anyway to make everyone happy — except for me.

I was very immature and unrealistic, incapable of building a good marriage. We had four children quickly even though hopes of getting away were constantly on my mind. When we did finally divorce, I quickly married again, making one bad choice after another. Guilt and shame grew in proportion to my mistakes even though I tried to deny what was happening. In my mind, I was a disgrace.

That's when the nightmares started. I presented myself well in public to people who knew nothing of my past, but all the mistakes couldn't be erased from my mind. Sessions with counselors through the years were helpful, especially my most recent therapist. It helped to confide in her and receive assurance that my past mistakes were no longer a factor; however, I couldn't move on. It was up to me to forgive myself and focus on the many gifts that were mine today. But the horrific dreams always returned.

I finally turned to God who was the one who gradually changed my thoughts and eventually my life. Spending time with him constantly, pouring out my heartache about the nightmares and laying them in his lap, slowly solved my problems. I never understood how he could love and forgive me when I couldn't do it for myself. He also surrounded me with loving Christians who shared their own struggles and healing. Their arms opened wide to greet me and walk this new life path with me. They continue to inspire, support, and love each other — and me now too — for who we are today; they don't care about yesterday. I finally learned from God and my new friends to release the past.

Now my days begin and end in prayer. My faith has never been stronger. Morning devotions prepare me for hours filled with positive thoughts and actions. Before going to sleep each night, I spend more quality time with God, often reading Scripture and some evenings just talking to him about little things. Always present is my desire to release negative thoughts from the past. As I focus on activities to help others and myself, there is no room for self-defeating thoughts to creep in. The nightmares have disappeared; now I wake up rested and ready to start the day with Jesus, my best friend and constant companion.

My hope is that you too can find peace and forgive yourself for past mistakes as you embrace each new day with the Lord as a fresh start. Each one is a priceless gift to treasure.

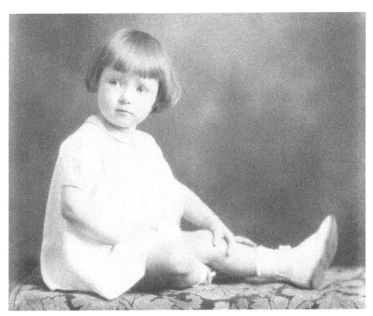

One of my few childhood photos (age 3).

Me with Mom and Dad on my wedding day.

Chapter 15
Dare to Strut Your Stuff

"This is a crazy idea! What was I thinking?" Those were among my thoughts as I walked toward the massive Kentucky Convention Center early on a November morning in 2019. There to audition for the *America's Got Talent* television show, along with 1200 other performers, I was certainly out of my comfort zone. Just because I had learned how to tap dance at 70 and was still doing it 20 years later didn't mean I could compete with professionals!

For some reason I was asked to try out after my daughter Diana sent *AGT* my tape and information. That didn't mean I had to accept their invitation or put myself out there to be embarrassed or have my feelings hurt. But I was not thinking about all of that when it came time to accept this opportunity. At first I thought this might make a good story or even inspire people my age to try new challenges, but now that it was actually happening, fear set in.

Fortunately, my husband Ed, Diana, and I had been given a card to bypass the long line of performers waiting around the block for their audition. "Was that because

I'm 90 and needed special help?" I wondered. We entered the stadium building without waiting and were immediately taken to a holding area, a designated spot in the auditorium.

Still afraid and intimidated, I stared wide-eyed at the number and diversity of the people with their acts all around me. (I learned later that there were hundreds of more contestants in other areas of the building — even from all over the world — who were there trying out.) What appeared to be about 20 Indians with real tomahawks were practicing their routine. One slip while they were dancing could have been fatal, but they seemed very relaxed. Everyone was dressed in costumes, some very elaborate and others bizarre. School bands were practicing as cheerleaders were thrown high in the air. Fortunately, they all landed safely. Half-naked acrobats were especially frightening, causing me to look away. Children dressed like adults danced together, ventriloquists ran through their routines with dummies on their laps, and many musicians in small groups practiced their songs as they waited. It was a busy, noisy scene.

After removing my coat, revealing a short cobalt-blue costume with matching feathered boa and headpiece, many of the people approached me wanting to take my picture. "Can we get a shot with you?" "I like your costume," "You're looking rad," were just a few of their comments. A news reporter requested an interview; the local television newswoman asked me to appear on her broadcast. This adventure was beginning to sink in. People were actually noticing me. It's going to make a *really* good story, I thought.

We weren't waiting long before an *AGT* staff member appeared, "We're ready for your audition; follow me downstairs," he said as we left the room. "This is it," I thought. I'll get it over with and just go home."

In the next waiting area, four groups of about 30 people each waited to audition. My group went in first and we were each given 90 seconds to perform our acts. As I watched the contestants ahead of me — some very good — I tried to stay calm. But when it was my turn, my heart began to race. I jumped up, went to the center, and then let it all go. There wasn't time to think about it. Tap dancing to "Sweet Gypsy Rose," I worked the boa and did as many burlesque moves as I could remember. The audition ended with a lot of attitude as I drug my boa offstage.

As we started to head back upstairs, I was stopped and asked to remain. After a short wait, another set of staff members took me to a nearby room and questioned me further; "Where do you dance professionally?" "Do you have an agent?" "Would you sign release papers?" They also wanted to see my dance. It was shocking that they would think I was a "real" dancer, but I performed my number, smiled a lot, and tried to look like a "professional." I signed release papers after that, then returned to the ballroom area. It all seemed so strange. I could only guess what was happening.

Other photographers took more pictures, and I was interviewed in the middle of the ballroom where I performed my dance again for a large crowd. The audience clapped, and the cameras zoomed in for close-ups. Everyone was staring and smiling. I could have been a nervous wreck. Luckily, there wasn't time.

Rushed to a huge lobby and talking with the newspaper reporter and television producer came next, in addition to more photos and a request that I dance again. "I learned to tap dance at 70 and started my own volunteer group with different kinds of performers," I told the reporter. "Now we entertain at senior residences in Carmel, Indiana, and 1 love what I'm doing." They said to look in the morning paper for an article and to watch the evening news, which would show my interview and dancing. "Is this really happening?" I asked myself again.

Back in the ballroom were groups of contestants waiting their turn and more visitors who wanted pictures. The cameras focused on me, panned the crowd, then came back. I managed to talk to other contestants who said, "We've tried out before, and we're not going to give up until we make it. Hardly anyone makes it on their first try." I did my best to encourage them.

The hours flew by until it was time to leave. But just before we did, Ed and I were asked to do a waltz in the middle of the dance floor and talk to each other about the day's experience — all while being filmed and recorded. "This has been a day to remember," I said at the end. Ed agreed.

The whole experience was surreal. We learned that those who made the final cut would be notified in January or February, and in March they would be flown to California for the next audition. I had my fingers, eyes, and toes crossed.

Remember my experience and don't be afraid to take a chance at any opportunity to share your talents and capabilities. You'll have special memories of it when you're 100 and telling your great-great-great grandchildren all about it. I intend to do exactly that!

Being interviewed by a reporter after my *AGT* audition.

Daughter Diana was with me every step of the way.

Chapter 16
Dare to Survive a Worldwide Pandemic

"You got it, Mom," Diana exclaimed. "LA, here we come!"

It was February of 2020, and my daughter had just been notified by the *America's Got Talent* producer that I had made it to the next audition in California. It was indeed a shock! Trying out last November had been a lot of fun, but despite the encouragement I had received from *AGT*, I never really expected to be chosen for the next cut. Now, the staff sent me an airline ticket, a song to use for my dance, lots of papers to sign, and more instructions to follow. I couldn't believe this was happening to me. Wow!

At the same time more and more news was reaching the public about a deadly virus spreading around the world — even here in the States — and later our own community. I was focused on practicing for my spring Follies show so the members would soon be ready to perform at retirement homes. However, a feeling of fear and anxiety gradually grew that affected everyone, and by mid-March, the reality of the highly contagious virus was causing changes in our world. By the end of the month, it was attacking millions of people and killing thousands, with the numbers rising daily.

A new reality was setting in: Everyone was told to wear masks and distance from each other, stores and restaurants were closing, schools were shifting to remote learning, church services were moving online, and many senior residences, where the Follies entertained, were "locked" down. Residents there were encouraged to remain in their own apartments, meals were delivered to them, and family visits were prohibited.

So, it was no surprise when the *AGT* producers cancelled the March auditions. Of course, it was disappointing, but I had no intention of flying to LA — at that time the hub of the Coronavirus — to perform. My thoughts and prayers were focused on the victims of the virus, not on my tap dancing for a television show.

Despite my disappointment I soon realized that God had other plans for me. He put it on my heart to reach out to isolated seniors by doing random acts of kindness, something my granddaughter Carolyn started years ago. Each day I sent encouraging cards or small gifts to people anonymously or called shut-ins just to chat and brighten their long days at home alone. It soon became the highlight of my day too.

Another "God thing" happened during the pandemic. It was time to begin that book I had wanted to write my whole life. For decades, it had been put aside because of other priorities. Now, with everything shut down, there were no excuses. Obligations were on hold, so it was time to begin my story. Guess where my writing happened — in a little "Pink Palace" (as I liked to call it). My palace, a spare room with the walls painted bubble gum pink is full of family pictures, keepsakes — memories from the past — and all of my favorite things (including dishes, of course). It was my cozy castle and a perfect place to begin this new journey.

You may recall from an earlier chapter that I was crowned queen of the Erma Bombeck Writers' Workshop and given a tiara, which I often wore while writing in the palace. Waking up every morning during the pandemic and knowing I could go to the Pink Palace and create my chapters for this book provided so much joy. Many people may feel that an active fulfilling life is over when they reach a certain age, and they can begin to shut down. Sharing my life experiences and the happiness I have discovered through the years is proof that this is not the best alternative.

When I wasn't writing chapters for this book, I was working on shorter essays and was published for a second time in *Chicken Soup for the Soul: Age Is Just a Number* edition. Since it was released during the pandemic and before the protection of vaccines, we had a socially distanced book signing on my daughter Julie's porch. We even had curbside pickup! It was fun to have friends drop by for a visit and book – and I sold out!

The pandemic also birthed a new slogan for a fun activity I do each week with my daughter Julie. During the quarantine, "Positivity from the Porch" was born! Two years before the virus arrived, we had created weekly

"Porchcasts," where we would sit on her porch for a short chat to provide our viewers with a message of inspiration — and sometimes a surprise tap dance! However, because of the virus I was unable to see Julie, and we had to shift our porchcasts to online — most of the time from the Pink Palace. We would broadcast every week with our new theme, "Positivity from the Porch" to inspire and encourage viewers to seek and share positive thoughts and actions during this difficult time. "Queen Lori and Princess Julie," along with mascot Toto, added humor with relevant messages and off-the-cuff chatter. It's been a fun new adventure and educational, too, as I learned new tools in the video world including BeLive and Zoom.

Being quarantined at home also gave me more time to grow in my faith. In addition to my usual morning devotions, I joined Julie's online Sunday evening Bible study which has not only enriched my understanding of God's Word but also strengthened me by uniting me with other Christians. Their peace and unconditional love is inspiring.

I know the best is yet to come! We will conquer this pandemic; vaccines are being rolled out as I type. The people lost from the virus will always be remembered, of course, along with the sacrifices of first responders, medical workers, and volunteers across the world.

Despite this worldwide tragedy, blessings came with it too. Our busy lives slowed down, families bonded with each other, and we discovered a new appreciation for home. We will never again take life for granted.

My book signing for *Chicken Soup for the Soul: Age Is Just a Number* was a huge success, and I sold over 50 books despite the pandemic.

At the book signing with assistant "Princess Elaine," we socially distanced on the porch.

Chapter 17
Dare to Pay It Forward

Here I sit, completing my book and amazed at what has transpired. If anyone would have told me that this could have happened, I would have said they were crazy, didn't know me, and certainly had no idea of my writing capabilities. But God knew and believed in me — and others did too. In fact, he never left my side even when the words wouldn't come, a whole chapter had to be dumped, or I doubted my own ability. What's even more amazing is that God not only provided what I needed to become a writer, but he equipped me to "Pay it Forward" to help others, even as I was in the process of learning to become one myself.

As I look back on how it all started — unexpectedly — at the Erma Bombeck Writers' Workshop when I was crowned queen and promised to return as an author, it seems unreal. Me, publicly announcing to hundreds of people that I would become a writer was a bold, unrealistic thing to say at the time — and that wasn't all. I had never used a computer before and was challenged by the thought of it.

As you have read in previous chapters, my daughter Julie got me started with baby steps, to at least be able to write pages in the correct format. We struggled on a jungle-like journey through technology to enable me to continue writing, putting down thoughts and events from my past that could possibly inspire others to move forward. Sharing my challenges and victories brought me more joy than I had ever imagined. As I continued to learn and apply new skills to my writing, the desire to help others do the same surfaced as well. I wanted to assist them to fulfill their goals, and the pandemic provided a perfect opportunity.

My first chance to pay it forward while in quarantine came through a dear friend and fellow Follies performer, Sandy, who had started writing a memoir 10 years earlier, one that described the challenges of living as a blind person in a sighted world. Her struggle to lead a normal life amidst daily challenges and prejudice was an inspiring story that I knew needed to be shared with the world. But she was stuck and didn't know how to move forward, so her story sat on the back burner for years.

I began with reading her chapters, which were alive with poignant descriptions, colorful settings, vivid vocabulary and important resources and information to share. I did not attempt to make any corrections or try to edit her eloquent work. My skills were not ready to suggest changes or corrections of any kind, especially since her writing talent was clearly superior to mine.

However, she needed encouragement and a connection

to restart her project. Sandy's inspiring memoir needed to be published, and my daughter and I were able to make a recommendation to a trustworthy publisher to get her closer to her dream. After reading samples of her work, our publisher not only agreed to work with her, but he found an editor for her too. Sandy's manuscript was now out of a drawer and one step closer to completion and publishing. And today I am happy to say that Sandy's book, *See? Living Blind in a Sighted World* is now published and on sale through Amazon!

Sandy has also looked for opportunities to submit short stories for writing contests and other media, along with enrolling in courses to improve her skills. She is a gifted writer but needed encouragement from a friend to be empowered to share it. "Like kerosene fuels fire, Lori encouraged me with her positive feedback on my book. I feel both honored and humbled," Sandy said. "Lori's book was a daunting project in itself, yet she gave so much of her time and herself to help me with mine."

Another blessing came to me by way of my daughter's friend Tammy. She courageously started college after a 35+-year gap in her education and a lifetime of disabilities from cerebral palsy. She struggled to learn new computer skills, along with English 101 for her first class. I was happy to refresh my own knowledge from a lifelong teaching career to sit at her side and guide her. At first she was very discouraged and overwhelmed and wanted to give up. Her initial attempts to complete assignments caused sleepless nights and ongoing anxiety. However, as we tackled assignments together and she became more familiar with requirements and the new technology, she began to find her groove. Encouragement and acknowledgment for small successes changed her attitude, and she began to excel.

Tammy is currently working very hard and has improved tremendously. Her goal is to finish her education, write a memoir, and use her knowledge at future speaking engagements to encourage others. In the meantime, she penned this heartfelt note to me:

"'Mama Lori' arrived in my life at just the right time, after returning to school after 37 years, and I was not at all prepared for what I was about to face. With my first course, English 101, I found myself overwhelmed, discouraged, and in a foreign environment that I could not understand. Then came Mama Lori, who worked tirelessly to teach me what the last 37 years of time had erased. Because of her selfless efforts, love, and sharing of her knowledge, I went from wanting to give up to now getting ready to complete my fourth course, English Composition. I may have started back with a C, but I am proud to share my current grade, an A. Because of the love and knowledge Mama shared, I can continue earning a degree and fulfilling a lifelong goal. She will forever be a key part of my success."

We may never know how we affect others. I had no idea that a few words of encouragement and time spent with Tammy and Sandy would empower them on their new ventures. We all have something to give — sometimes it's encouragement and just being present. There are so many people with dreams to uncover and share who just need someone to believe in them and encourage them on their journey. And maybe that person is you.

Who would have guessed I could have helped someone with her book while I was still learning and writing mine? Or guided a new friend through a writing class and technology issues that I still struggle with every day? Any time there's a possibility of providing a helping hand, my heart tells me to go for it.

"Paying it Forward" brings joy to the giver as well as the receiver. Try it, and you'll see.

When Sandy Fortier is not writing,
she's performing with The Prime Life Follies.

Tammy Graham continues to thrive with her studies
and is loving every minute of it.

Chapter 18
Dare to Embrace Grandparenting

This chapter is dedicated to grandparents of all kinds: current ones, expectant ones, wannabes, and even those who have no desire to be grandparents but just want a few laughs!

Do you know what being a grandparent is? It's a reward for being a parent. Yes, and the first perk might even be your presence in the delivery room. Witnessing a miracle is hard to beat; there are no words to describe a life being birthed right before your eyes. You also get to celebrate a new baby boy or girl in your life without the anticipation of sleepless nights and other struggles of parenting that follow a baby's arrival. True, you may receive daily phone calls from your children when the baby is crying and they can't get him or her (or them; yes, twins in my case) to stop. Sometimes these calls are dialed in desperation. I actually received one from a son-in-law living in Japan! It feels good to know that our children finally acknowledge they need us and our wisdom; something they never did when, as teenagers, they thought they knew everything. Now they seek our counsel, realizing we did a pretty good job of parenting. After all, we raised *them*!

I was called into service many times as my grandbabies were born all over the world. With three daughters who seemed to have one baby right after another for a while, and a total of 18 grandchildren, I was definitely in demand.

"Grammie's Grab Bag" always traveled with me, starting when those babies became toddlers. And it worked every time. Marbles, crayons, coloring books, jacks, etc., were all "good behavior awards" when I left. Picking from the bag became the highlight of my visits for the children. And of course, it was not a bribe!

"Dancing Grammie," as I had been called since becoming a tap dancer at 70, loved being in charge of the baby and siblings — but no night duty for me. That's when I got rejuvenated for the next day. As the children grew older, we played games such as *Battleship* and *Uno*, watched *Mister Rogers' Neighborhood* and *Sesame Street*, did paintings and other crafts on the kitchen table and had one other favorite activity: we created and practiced "shows" for Mommy and Daddy. I taught my granddaughters some tap steps and put together performances with lots of twirling and leaping until the children got dizzy and plopped on the couch, abruptly ending the show. They had costumes made with strips of sequins from the ones I wore, and they really enjoyed that. I should mention the younger boys loved "dancing" too, and the older ones played the music and acted as MC for the show.

When I think about my days with the grandchildren, it reminds me of a busy hub of activity happening all around, with me in the middle of it. There was always a game going on, crafts covering the table and beyond, and children chattering and laughing. One time that laughter centered on little Will (my youngest grandson) as he crawled into the dog cage with Millie, the family dog (who was larger than Will). Never a dull minute, but it was lots of fun.

Dancing Grammie attended numerous birthday parties, First Communions, school programs, sporting events and graduations. I also jumped in many inflatables without breaking an arm or leg and went trick-or-treating dressed as Dorothy from *The Wizard of Oz*. I had to move pretty fast to keep up with the kids running from door-to-door. In addition, no one has likely pinned more tails on donkeys than I have.

My visits were limited to the States until one of my daughters, Julie, and her husband and 2-year-old son, Nathaniel, moved to Japan. Their daughter, Carolyn, was born there, and that trip was especially memorable because it took place during cherry blossom season. I had time to immerse myself in Japanese culture and spent many days with my grandchildren in a huge sandbox near their home. Julie actually taught me a trick for crying babies during that visit. We "fluffed" Carolyn on top of the dryer in her bassinet, and she fell asleep instantly. I soaked up plenty of special memories to take home with me, and the picture of Nathaniel bowing in his tiny kimono while saying "Arigato" is still vivid in my mind. Even little Carolyn helping him build Lego creations with her tiny fingers was a beautiful sight.

Just as memorable were my visits to other grandchildren who were physically closer — at least in the States. We celebrated holidays together, and it was always a wild scene. Each time, after stuffing ourselves with turkey and all the trimmings, the games began. One favorite was the white elephant gift exchange where everyone took a number and had a chance to pick something on his/her turn or "steal" a gift from someone else. Since I was the matriarch, no one attempted to take my gift, especially when it was chocolate. We enjoyed many laughs and created special memories.

Another trip I'll never forget was when I visited my oldest son and his family in New Jersey for Thanksgiving. My son Tom, a marathon runner, entered me in a 1-mile race called "The Turkey Trot" for my first venture into competitive sports. He and my 4-year-old granddaughter Jacqueline were running too. All I recall is that I came in last place with another woman who talked with me the entire way. Tom ranked among the winners, and even tiny Jacqueline surprised everyone with her speed, easily beating me to the finish. In fact, she has followed in her father's footsteps — not her grandmother's — and just completed the Boston Marathon.

As the "grands" grew up and got married, the "greats" began to appear on the scene. Distance and other factors such as busy work schedules made it difficult to get together. However, handmade "pictures" from the little ones often arrived in the mail, and during the pandemic we started to have "Zoom" visits that really helped us to stay connected. We are all anxious to be together again when it's safe. Plenty of hugs and kisses are being stored up by Gigi, as the "greats" call me these days.

Now for those of you who may not have biological grandchildren and would like to get in on all the fun, I have a potential solution for you. The senior living community where I live teams up with local school-age children to act as grandchildren for residents; and from what I can see, everyone involved loves it. Many have frequent get-togethers, and for those who want to spend even more time with one another, they make their own individual arrangements. I've seen them dining together, going on outings or just playing games as they visit. It's a win-win situation and a beautiful sight to see.

This all began with an "Adopt a Grandparent" program at senior centers or residences and school districts around the country, so check out the programs in your area. A phone call may be all that is needed to join this rewarding venture where you live. I have a hunch many facilities and schools will be eager to restart more social activities like this once we are beyond the pandemic.

Among the many things I treasure in my life, grand-parenting is high on the list. How about joining me for the fun!

Some of my grandchildren at our 2000 family reunion.

There's lots of laughter and fun with my
great-grandchildren (from bottom to top):
Thomas, Connor, Rowan, and Ford.

Chapter 19
Dare to Stay Alive

As I opened my eyes and looked around, confusion set in. I didn't know where I was. There was a large tube down my throat, so I couldn't even ask. Lying motionless in a hospital bed scared me. Was I dying? What happened to me?

As I regained consciousness, the nurses tried to communicate, telling me that this was the intensive care unit where I had been sent after a fall the day before. The last thing I could remember was leaving the doctor's office after a routine check-up and walking toward my car in the rain. The torrential downpour drenched me, and gusting winds that sounded like a tornado were coming right at me.

Next, I woke up with doctors and nurses examining me in the emergency room. At one point I tried to get up, but slipped out of the bed, causing a large gash on my forehead. That was just the beginning. After a series of uncomfortable X-rays, the medical team discovered that my pelvis was broken and there was internal bleeding. After that diagnosis, an ambulance immediately whisked me away to the local trauma hospital.

Constant monitoring revealed that my blood pressure had dropped to a dangerous level and my heart was unstable, so preparations were made for surgery. Numerous blood transfusions took place as friends and family members began to arrive. Many others were already praying. My good friend and pastor, Dr. Joan Malick, led the surgical team in a prayer before they started, so even though I didn't know it at the time, my life was in good hands.

As the sedation for surgery set in, I could feel myself drifting off and feeling as if my body was in a strange new place whirling around inside a capsule. I desperately wanted to get out. That finally stopped, a bright light appeared, and someone who I believe was God took my hand and led me back to my hospital bed. It was at that moment that I knew my life was saved and my remarkable recovery began. I also found out later that when the doctor had gone in to stop the internal bleeding, it had already stopped on its own. Prayers were being heard. God was already at work healing me.

As I lay in the ICU and family members arrived, I was more coherent and aware of what was happening. I tried to talk through the ventilator but realized my attempts were futile. As I became more stabilized the next day, the ventilator was removed from my throat allowing me to talk, another sign of my improving condition that provided hope.

Strong drugs were still being administered to lessen the intense pain from my pelvis break; however, after a few days in the ICU, all the tubes and lines were removed and I was transferred to the orthopedic unit. In this area, which was in a different wing, there was more emphasis on rehabilitation and therapy. Now I was far removed from the pampering and attention received earlier, but it offered my first step back toward independence and being well again, and I soon adjusted to the reality. My goal was to get home and back to normal.

I spent a week receiving basic therapy, mainly assistance with getting out of bed and standing up, and was then transferred to a rehabilitation hospital for another 12 days to have daily therapeutic exercises to strengthen and get me walking again.

No time was wasted getting started in this intensive rehabilitation program. On the first day at 7:30 a.m., my physical therapist, Jordayn, wheeled me to their large gymnasium and began to work on my legs. I couldn't recall using them for a long time. But by the time the hour-long session ended, I was able to use a walker, putting one foot in front of the other and placing each leg slowly ahead. With the extreme pelvis pain, just moving my body was a fete, but little by little getting in and out of a chair and bed even became easier. I graduated to skills such as climbing up and down stairs and getting in and out of a mock car. I also picked up lots of cups off of the floor while maneuvering my walker around them. Jordayn was so encouraging and would brag about me frequently. "Lori, you're doing better than my 23-year-old patient with the same fracture," she said. That made me laugh and empowered me to walk more than 200 feet for her before leaving. It was hard to tell her "Goodbye."

My occupational therapist, McKenzie, also contributed to my success. She showed up every morning with a positive "You can do it" attitude, teaching me to easily navigate daily tasks during recovery. She also gave me my first shower in several weeks, found the most comfortable chair for me to use, and prepared me for tasks at home. She was indeed a joy.

A nurse named Shawn also deserves extra credit for her kind and encouraging attitude every night of my stay in rehab. Her caring attitude and excellent skills made me feel safe and loved. There were other special nurses and a therapist named Bob in the ortho unit who was so tender transferring my painful body to X-rays and scans. Kindness goes a long way when you are hurting.

After over a week in the rehabilitation hospital, I had made tremendous progress and met my discharge goals. Unfortunately, though, there was a setback that occurred a few days before my release. I fell during the night when an aide was assisting me to the bathroom. The staff immediately sent me to the trauma hospital for X-rays and to check out a new cut on my forehead that wouldn't stop bleeding due to the blood thinner I was taking. Everything checked out OK, so I was sent back to the rehabilitation hospital and then home two days later.

Upon returning home, my daughters Diana and Maria, along with my daughter-in-law Beth, took turns staying with me, getting up at night when necessary and holding me when using the walker to get around the house, totally spoiling me for a few weeks. My son Tom also flew in during my hospital stay to be with me, and special friend Mark jumped in to help with airport transportation for family, favorite meals, and wherever he was needed. Adopted daughter Kandice showed up immediately at the hospital and never left my side, sharing Scripture, songs, and prayers. Finally, my daughter Julie, who had flown back from Florida when I was in the ICU, continues to assist me now in many ways and is always there for me. My path to healing was a team effort from the start.

Home therapy was an important part of my recovery with both physical and occupational therapists visiting twice a week to practice strength-building skills using the walker around the house and even outside. Rodger and Josue gave me exercises to do on my own, and I saw improvement all the time. I know I would not be able to walk now without these caring and loving therapists.

As I reflect on the accident and remarkable recovery, there are many to thank starting with God, of course. None of this would have been possible without the prayers and support of family, friends, and many outstanding medical staff members, both in the hospital and at home. Also, having my loved ones by my side as I took each step made all the difference in my recovery. To say I was cared for and loved back to life is truly an understatement.

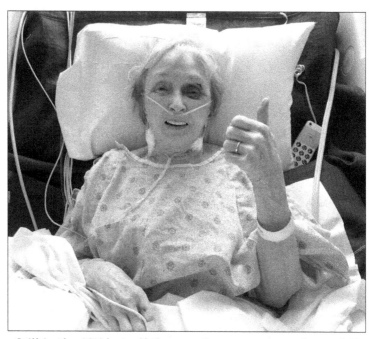

Still in the ICU but off the ventilator two days after a fall
that broke my pelvis and caused internal bleeding.

My therapists in rehab got me up and walking right away.
I'll be back in my tap dancing shoes soon!

Chapter 20
Dare to Live Joyfully Ever After

It's hard to end this book because I feel like my life is just getting started. Through the pages of my story, I hope you were inspired to see that it's never too late to fulfill your dreams and share them with others. No matter where you are in life, you can start something new — right now.

As you read in chapter one, my journey began after a traumatic period of loss, when I was ready to give up. It was then that God stepped in and redirected me onto a new path. He led me on many unexpected adventures that brought joy — some that even made me laugh out loud again when they popped up as I was writing this book. It was fun to reminisce about the start of a new career at 87, not to mention becoming Dancing Grammie, which was the biggest surprise of all and has brought more joy to me and others than I could have ever imagined. It still does.

But there were many struggles along the way. Letting go of people I loved, things I cherished, and trusting that God would be there was not easy. And then there was technology! Maybe the sequel to this book will be about the daily challenges that continue when I log on to my computer — *Dare to Survive the Computer* has a good ring to it. I've just met someone called "Siri," so now I have a partner in crime.

Emotionally there were barriers too. Writing about my son's death, the decline of my husband's health and his passing, and then my very recent visit to the ICU made me relive these difficult times all over again. I survived those, and also writing about them, by turning the painful tasks over to the Lord so he could assist me. I had never done that before, but it brought peace. I know now that I'm never alone.

When God took up residence in my heart during those times, life took on new meaning. It wasn't self-centered as before; it was God-centered. My faith also led me to become the joy-filled person I am today, surrounded by people who dedicate their lives in the same way.

My plan for the future is to continue living a simple life, waking up each morning in my little cottage to start the day with devotions and writing. Volunteering with The Follies and participating in other service activities will always be a part of my days. Perhaps teaching a simple class of beginning computer skills for people like me might be a good addition too. God has equipped me with the time and basic knowledge now to help others, and I want to continue. The rewards are life changing.

As I close this chapter of my life and book, here are some thoughts that helped me on my journey that I want to leave with you:

- Live gratefully. Each day is a gift.
- Don't go on this journey alone. God is with you, so take him along.
- Get started, have a plan, change it if necessary.
- Remember your past. Learn from it, then leave it behind.
- Take risks. You won't know if you don't try.
- Get help when you need it. We're not meant to struggle alone.
- Carve out time every day for your passion. Don't let the fire go out.
- Be open to new things. Technology won't kill you (even if you want to kill it).
- Never give up. Sometimes you have to step away to regroup.
- Expect obstacles. Don't let them derail you.
- Live a life beyond yourself. You will never regret it.
- Above all, don't forget to praise God, trusting him every step of the way.

And now it's time for you to
"Dare to live joyfully ever after!"

I'm back on the porch and ready for my next dance
and chapter. The best is yet to come!

About the Author

"It's never too late" is my mantra, and at 92 I'm not slowing down. I am a mother of seven, grandmother of twenty-two, and a retired schoolteacher. But my dream has always been to be a writer. And it happened – at the age of 87! My writing career began the moment I was crowned Queen of the 2016 Erma Bombeck Writers' Workshop. Since then, my work has appeared twice in the popular *Chicken Soup for the Soul* series: *Grandparents* and *Age Is Just a Number* editions. And what you're holding now is my first book (but not my last).

When I'm not writing, you will find me tap dancing at local retirement communities as founder of The Prime Life Follies, a volunteer group my late husband and I started in 2003 to bring joy to shut-ins and residents.

You may also catch me dancing and sharing life lessons on weekly "Porchcasts" with my daughter, Julie Osborne. Our goal is to share "Positivity from the Porch," and we hope you check us out on my website at www.DancingGrammie.com.

At 92, this queen is just getting started! "The best is yet to come."

- *Dancing Grammie*

Contact Me

I would love to hear from you! The best way to reach me is through email:

DancingGrammieLori@gmail.com

If you enjoyed *Dare to Live* and would like to read more of my stories or tune into our "Porchcasts" for some "Positivity from the Porch," you can find them on my website at www.DancingGrammie.com. You can also sign up there for our weekly newsletter.

And, I've heard that it helps new writers like me to build a platform (whatever that is), so please leave me a review on Amazon and follow me on The Facebook:

www.Facebook.com/DancinGrammie

That's all of the technology that I've learned so far, but I've heard of something called "Tweeting" that sounds fun, so stay tuned.

I hope to hear from you soon!

~ *Dancing Grammie*

CPSIA information can be obtained
at www.ICGtesting.com
Printed in the USA
LVHW050834231121
704194LV00003B/9